1
Introducing Botswana

With its unspoiled wildernesses and promise of adventure, Botswana is one of the last remaining safari destinations in Africa where you can still experience nature as the early explorers did.

This magnificent country boasts a treasure trove of options for the tourist, from the famous **Okavango Delta** wetlands to the incredible **Makgadikgadi salt pans**, from grass plains of migrating zebra to the stark openness of the **Kalahari** and the huge herds of elephant in **Chobe**.

Botswana is one of the world's most thinly populated countries with less than 3 people per km² (5 per sq mile), and at independence in 1966 it was also one of the poorest. However, since then there has been remarkable growth in all sectors of the economy, including tourism, conservation and wildlife management.

With almost 20% of the country protected as national park or wildlife management area, Botswana has made a real commitment to conservation, and many of its people have now begun to appreciate the value of managed conservation areas. The Nata Sanctuary was one of the first examples of how the local population can financially benefit from the administration of their own wildlife areas. Although, unlike most other African countries, this trend has been evident in Botswana since the early 1960s, when the Batawana people agreed that their traditional hunting grounds in the Okavango should be protected. This act was hailed as a landmark in African tribal history and the area was named the Moremi Game Reserve after the late Chief Moremi III.

TOP ATTRACTIONS

*** **The Okavango:** mokoro trails, game viewing, walking safaris, fishing.
*** **The Chobe:** elephant, fishing, birding and game viewing.
*** **The Makgadikgadi:** exploring, driving, camping, flamingoes.
** **The Kalahari:** lions, gemsbok, vast unspoiled landscapes.
** **Tuli:** night drives, walking safaris, leopard, hyena, elephant.

Opposite: *A baobab tree mirrored in the waters of the Okavango.*

THE LAND

Located in the centre of southern Africa and covering an area of 581,730km² (224,548 sq miles), Botswana is a landlocked country, just slightly smaller than the U.S. state of Texas. Namibia lies to the west and north of the country with the thin Caprivi Strip which runs along the top of Botswana. While to the south lies South Africa and to the east there is Zimbabwe. In the northwest for just 700m (765yd) Botswana and Zambia meet along the world's shortest international boundary.

Extending through nine degrees of latitude, two thirds of the country lies within the **tropics**, but unlike most 'tropical' countries, Botswana is dry and prone to drought. The vast **Kalahari Desert**, the largest continuous stretch of sand in the world, covers 84% of Botswana, extending from the Orange River in South Africa to the equator in Gabon.

When the supercontinent of Gondwana started breaking up about 200 million years ago, a series of three basins was formed through the middle of central and southern Africa. The Kalahari Basin was the last of these, and it is now almost completely full of aeolian sand, levelling the country to an average height of 950m (3117ft) above sea level.

Granite gneiss rocks formed the base of this original basin, which is now covered by up to 200m (656ft) of sand, but along the borders of the country, particularly around Francistown and in the southern Barolong area, fragments of these ancient rocks – possibly the oldest rocks in the world at more than 3.5 billion years of age – can still be found. Overlaying this deeply buried foundation stone is a matrix of Karoo deposits made up of sandstone, basalt lavas, shales and thin seams of coal, all about 300 million years old.

GLOBETROTTER™
Travel Guide

BOTSWANA

ALAN BROUGH

NEW
HOLLAND

NEW
HOLLAND

★★★ Highly recommended
★★ Recommended
★ See if you can

Fourth edition published in 2006
by New Holland (Publishers) Ltd
London • Cape Town • Sydney • Singapore
First edition published in 1997

10 9 8 7 6 5 4 3 2

website: www.newhollandpublishers.com

Garfield House, 86 Edgware Road
London W2 2EA, United Kingdom

80 McKenzie Street
Cape Town 8001, South Africa

14 Aquatic Drive, Frenchs Forest,
NSW 2086, Australia

218 Lake Road, Northcote,
Auckland, New Zealand

Distributed in the USA by
The Globe Pequot Press, Connecticut

ISBN 978 1 84537 596 6

Although every effort has been made to ensure that this
guide is up to date and current at time of going to print,
the Publisher accepts no responsibility or liability for
any loss, injury or inconvenience incurred by readers
or travellers using this guide.

Keep us Current
Information in travel guides is apt to change, which is why
we regularly update our guides. We'd be grateful to receive
feedback if you've noted something we should include in
our updates. If you have new information, please share it
with us by writing to the Publishing Manager, Globetrotter,
at the office nearest to you (addresses on this page). The
most significant contribution to each new edition will
receive a free copy of the updated guide.

Publishing Manager): Thea Grobbelaar
DTP Cartographic Manager: Genené Hart
Editors: Thea Grobbelaar, Melany McCallum, Laurence
Lemmon-Warde, Anouska Good
Cartographers: Genené Hart, Marisa Galloway,
John Hall, Eloise Moss
Design and DTP: Nicole Bannister, Laurence Lemmon-
Warde, Sonya Cupido
Compiler/Verifier: Elaine Fick

Reproduction by Hirt & Carter (Pty) Ltd, Cape Town.
Printed and bound by Times Offset (M) Sdn. Bhd., Malaysia.

Acknowledgments: The author would like to express his
appreciation to GEAR-V Adventures and the management
and staff of Okavango Wilderness Safaris, whose generous
support has greatly enhanced the content of this book.
Their standard of professional conduct and environmental
concern in ensuring the long-term sustainable development of Botswana's outstanding tourist attractions for all
its visitors are exemplary.

Photographic Credits:
Daryl Balfour, title page, pages 8–10, 12, 18, 19, 22, 23,
25, 28, 29, 30, 33, 35, 37, 38, 52, 59, 60, 62, 64, 66,
69–72, 78, 82, 85, 86, 88, 91, 92 (bottom), 93–102, 106,
112, 113, 116, 117 (top), 119; **Daryl and Sharna
Balfour/IOA**, 58; **Michael Brett**, pages 7, 44, 47–49, 75,
81, 84; **Cape Archives** (Depot), pages 15, 16; **Nigel J
Dennis/IOA**, 56; **Bev Flinn**, page 50; **Roger de la
Harpe/IOA**, page 103 (top and bottom); **Martin
Harvey/IOA**, cover; **Leonard Hoffman/IOA**, pages 13, 73;
Illustrative Options, pages 11, 14, 20, 21, 24, 26, 39, 40,
55, 57, 61, 63, 74, 83, 92 (top), 110, 111, 114, 115, 118;
Ian Michler/IOA, 4; **Ulf Nermark/Activepic**, 34; **Peter
Pickford/IOA**, pages 27, 41, 117 (bottom); **Colour
Library/IOA**, page 6.
[*IOA: Images of Africa*]

Cover: *A mokoro glides tourists lazily across a lodge's
lawn, deep in the Okavango Delta.*
Title page: *A herd of buffalo (*Syncerus caffer*) gallop
across shallow lagoons in the Okavango Delta.*

CONTENTS

One of Botswana's more recent – and more fortunate – geological events was the eruption of several **kimberlitic volcanic pipes** which punched through the earth's crust some 80 million years ago. Under the right temperature and pressure conditions the carbon contained in some of these lavas changed over a long period of time into the **diamonds** which today fuel Botswana's economic development.

Above: *A blowing sandstorm dusts down the Kalahari just before the summer rains break.*
Opposite: *The characteristic red dunes of the Kgalagadi Transfrontier Park.*

While Botswana is often depicted as being a flat featureless semidesert, there is much wonder and variation to be found in this vast land. One of the greatest paradoxes this arid sandveld encompasses is the lush, verdant jewel of the **Okavango Delta** formed as the wide, fast-flowing Okavango River spills out across a massive area of sand where it eventually soaks away, drying up in its futile search for the sea.

Other remarkable features punctuating Botswana's terrain include the immense **Makgadikgadi pans**, whose salt-cracked surface marks the death bed of the great Lake Makgadikgadi. Along the eastern edge of the country, the landscape has more variety with hills and *kopjes* (rocky mounds), while in the far west and southwest, deep in the Kalahari, the terrain is completely flat and arid.

Climate

As is typical of deserts far from the moderating influence of the sea, and as the country extends over nine degrees of latitude, there is considerable variation in the seasons and climatic conditions in Botswana.

COMPARATIVE CLIMATE CHART	GABORONE				FRANCISTOWN				MAUN			
	SUM	AUT	WIN	SPR	SUM	AUT	WIN	SPR	SUM	AUT	WIN	SPR
	JAN	APR	JUL	OCT	JAN	APR	JUL	OCT	JAN	APR	JULY	OCT
MIN TEMP. °C	20	13	4	16	19	14	5	16	20	16	7	19
MAX TEMP. °C	33	27	23	31	31	28	23	31	33	32	26	36
MIN TEMP. °F	68	55	39	61	66	57	41	61	68	61	45	66
MAX TEMP. °F	91	81	73	88	88	82	73	88	91	90	79	97
HOURS OF SUN	9	7.9	9.7	9.3	8.5	8.4	9.7	9.2	8.4	9	10	9.2
RAINFALL mm	104	50	4	46	99	28	0	31	112	27	0	19
RAINFALL in	4.1	2	0.2	1.8	3.9	1.1	0	1.2	4.4	1.1	0	0.7

PRECIOUS WATER

The vital importance of water to Botswana is reflected in the fact that the local monetary currency is called *Pula* and *Thebe*, which in Setswana means 'rain' and 'drops'. In this country of continual drought, rain and wealth are considered to be one and the same.

Opposite: *The golden grasslands of the Central Kalahari Game Reserve stretch away as far as the eye can see.*
Below: *The tranquil waters of the Chobe River reflect the dying embers of the sun at dusk.*

There are generally only two seasons: summer, which lasts from October to April; and winter which is slightly shorter, from May to September. The vast majority of rain falls between December and February, although even during this period there can be long dry spells when temperatures can soar to over 40°C (104°F). In winter the night temperatures can plummet to below freezing. But at any time of year, be it midwinter or midsummer, visitors can generally count on sunny clear blue skies with very few consistently cloudy days.

Rainfall is often in the form of short, sharp thunderstorms followed by sunshine, which, while good for tourists, is detrimental to farmers as it causes much of the precipitation to evaporate before it can soak into the soil. The quantity and reliability of rainfall decreases from the northeast of the country, where 600mm (24in) can be expected with a variability of 30%, to the southwest, where an annual rainfall of only 200mm (8in) can be expected with a variability of 80%.

Rivers and Mountains

Apart from the **Okavango River** there is no other perennial water supply flowing into, or out of, Botswana. Only the **Chobe River** in the extreme north, which separates Botswana from Namibia's Caprivi Strip flows all year round. For this reason, water is one of Botswana's most precious commodities and there is grave concern about its availability for a growing population in the near future.

The Chobe, Okavango and Zambezi rivers all have their source in the rain-drenched eastern Angolan highlands, where there is an average annual rainfall of well over 1200mm (47in). Under dif-

ferent names the Chobe and Okavango rivers meander in a parallel course southwards through Angola to cross Namibia's Caprivi Strip. At Mohembo just north of Shakawe the Okavango enters Botswana having changed its name from the Cuito River. For a further 90km (54 miles) the wide fast-flowing Okavango is hemmed in a narrow floodplain between two parallel fault lines until it pours into the flat Kalahari sand to fan out across the expanse of the Okavango Delta.

The **Thamalakane River** drains the Okavango Delta, carrying the minuscule overflow through Maun. The two main rivers that drain the east of the country are the **Shashe** and the **Motloutse**. The seasonal flow of the Motloutse has now been dammed to provide water for the towns of eastern Botswana through a massive pipeline stretching across 360km (216 miles) of dry countryside.

Much of the country is flat, savanna grassland with a scattering of thorn and scrub bush, although the south-eastern hardveld has a somewhat varied geology with more reliable rainfall, greater fertility and agricultural potential. As a result, 80% of the country's population lives in this region.

This more densely populated swathe of land constitutes just 20% of the country and runs from Ramokgwebana at the border with Zimbabwe in the

RIVER OF MANY NAMES

The Chobe River crosses the Caprivi Strip just under 200km (120 miles) east of the Okavango River, but does not actually enter the country; instead this wide watercourse defines the international border between Botswana and Namibia. The Chobe starts its life in Angola as the Kwando River, then becomes the Linyanti as it passes through the Caprivi and feeds the Linyanti Swamps. For a short stretch just before Lake Liambezi it is known as the Itenge, before finally becoming the Chobe.

Above: *The famous 'Van der Post's Panel' of ancient bushman paintings in the Tsodilo Hills.*

TREASURE-TROVE TUNNELS

Overlooking the dunes on Botswana's far western border are the Gcwihaba Hills, in which hide the mysterious Drotsky's Caverns. Shown to Martinus Drotsky by the Bushmen in 1934, these dramatic caverns are the result of climate changes which, over the eons, have carved out the passages and formed the fantastic flowstones, stalagmites and stalactites. Legend has it that the founder of Ghanzi, Hendrik van Zyl hid his huge fortune of gold and ivory in these caves before he was tried for murder. After his death the treasure was never found and, as yet, these caves remain fully unexplored.

east to Ramatlabama on the South African border near Mafikeng in the south. Along its length, hilly ranges and rocky outcrops adorn the landscape.

There are no **mountains** in Botswana and, apart from the hilly southeast, the only hills of significance are found in the northwest where there are three outcrops. Located in a flat sea of sand, these ranges are of geological and historical significance.

The most important of these is the **Tsodilo Hills** whose rocky cliffs rise up about 400m (1312ft) above the surrounding plain, and can be seen from the Okavango Delta over 50km (31 miles) away. The Tsodilo Hills are one of the most significant historical rock art sites in the world with as many as 3500 individual paintings charting over 25,000 years of almost continual human habitation in the area.

The **Aha** and **Gcwihaba** hills are approximately 150km (90 miles) south of Tsodilo and are extremely remote, involving a difficult 10–12 hour journey by four-wheel-drive vehicle to reach them. Although *Aha* means 'little rocks', these hills form the largest range in northern Botswana, overlooking the dune fields of the Namibian border.

The **Gcwihaba Hills** to the east are part of the same range and are named after an ancient river which used to flow through them. *Gcwihaba* is the !Kung word for 'hyena's lair', and it was this river that created the magnificent **Drotsky's Caverns** with their dramatic stalagmites, stalactites and flowstone formations which are also to be found in the range. !Kung is an almost forgotten San (Bushman) dialect spoken in northwestern Botswana.

Inland Waters

As an arid semidesert country with very little usable surface water, it is remarkable that in years of good rain Botswana can suddenly be blessed with immense shallow sheets of water as the huge northern salt pans fill up.

The inflow of the Okavango River alone would be enough to support the needs of a fully industrialized nation, were it not for evaporation. Unfortunately the pressure to harness this water is great – Angola needs the water to set up agricultural projects and Namibia wants to dam the watercourse. However, if the unique river flow is reduced or disturbed in any way, much of the Delta could be threatened. Consequently there is continual lobbying by conservation groups for greater protection of the Delta.

While completely dry for much of the year the major Makgadikgadi pans of **Sowa**, **Ntwetwe** and **Nxai**, with their countless smaller companions, do fill with both local rainfall and the inflow of certain rivers such as the Nata and Boteti. As the pans are clay-bottomed, the water is not readily absorbed into the ground and often remains on the surface long into the winter, when the pans become focal points for thirsty birds and wildlife.

These pans are actually the last remains of the great inland lake that covered much of northern Botswana 40,000 years ago. It was fed by the combined inflow of

PRECIOUS WATER

Water is extremely valuable in this dry country and the entire country's development hinges on its availability. This vulnerability was cruelly driven home during the droughts of 1983–1987 and 2004–2006 when water shortages brought national development to a standstill. To guard against this, in the 1990s the government undertook the largest construction project ever in Botswana to pipe water from a dam on the Motloutse River to supply over 50% of the country's population. But the ever-increasing demand for water is already outstripping this supply, and new sources need to be found and developed.

Below: *Palms on Chief's Island stand silhouetted against the rising sun.*

FISHING

The north of Botswana is a fisherman's paradise. The resorts at Shakawe in the Okavango Panhandle are famous for **tigerfish** and **bream**, and the length of the Chobe River offers excellent sport fishing. An annual event not to be missed in the northern Okavango near the Panhandle is the '**Barbel Run**'. This occurs between September and October when masses of small fish are forced to swim upstream as the floodplains dry up. The **catfish** (or barbel as they are known locally) attack them in a feeding frenzy, which in turn attracts crocodiles who feed on the catfish. An unforgettable spectacle for both fishermen and photographers.

the Okavango, Chobe and Zambezi rivers, spanning an area of up to 60,000km² (23,160 sq miles) to a maximum depth of 100m (328ft). This area is at the tail end of the Great East African Rift Valley and, being tectonically unstable, the faulting and warping of the earth's crust over the centuries diverted both the Chobe and Zambezi rivers causing the superlake to dry up.

As recently as 1500 years ago there was still water in the lowest levels of the lake, but today all that remains is a flat, sun-baked parchland called the **Makgadikgadi**. Covering 12,000 km² (4632 sq miles) the pans which make up the Makgadikgadi are absolutely featureless, without a single rock or blade of grass. It is this very desolation that has made them into such a tourist attraction, but the pans are also of economic importance: vast deposits of brine are being extracted from Sowa Pan for the production of not only salt, but also soda ash for use by the world's glass and chemical manufacturers.

The Animal Kingdom

Botswana's prime attraction is its abundant bird and wildlife. Over 160 different mammal species have been identified, including the 'big five' – **lion**, **leopard**, **elephant**, **buffalo** and **rhino** – as well as a myriad antelope including the rare aquatic **sitatunga** and **red lechwe**.

Below: *Africa's most endangered carnivore, the wild dog, hunts in packs.*

Over 550 **bird** species have been identified, 400 of which can be seen in the Gaborone area. Several of these birds are extremely rare and are unique to certain areas of Botswana. The best 'birding' areas are the Okavango Delta, the Chobe River from Kazungula to Serondela, the Tuli area, and Nata while an incredible array of raptors can be seen in the Mabuasehube area of the Kgalagadi Transfrontier Park. The best time of year for bird-watching is during the hot summer months when males sport their bright breeding plumage and droves of migrants have arrived.

Although generally shy and seldom encountered, **snakes** remain a concern for tourists and campers. Of the 72 species found in Botswana only 15 are dangerous, and just half of these are deadly. On the other hand, you are likely to see some of the 157 different reptiles and amphibians, particularly crocodiles, lizards, geckos, monitors and frogs.

A bewildering array of flying and crawling insects are to be found in Botswana, but few of them are dangerous or unpleasant. Contrary to popular belief, the most dangerous creatures you are likely to see on your trip are not lions or buffalo, but **mosquitoes**. Antimalaria precautions must be taken.

With their painful bite, **tsetse fly** can also be very trying, particularly in the summer months, but one should not forget that it has been their presence that has saved the Okavango from the cattle onslaught. **Scorpions** can also add an unpleasant sting to your trip, so it's a good idea to shake out your shoes before putting them on. They are not deadly and ordinary antihistamine cream provides effective relief, so be sure to pack a tube!

While there are some really impressive **spiders** in Botswana – the fearsome button spider, the eight-eyed jumping spider and the incredible 'golden orb' spider which spins an iridescent golden thread – the only spider that might bite (an unlikely occurrence), and which is responsible for 90% of spider bites in southern Africa, is the innocent-looking little 'sac spider' which spins a noticeable smudgy white nest on curtains and in cupboards. Its painless bite is cytotoxic.

Above: *The large granulated rock scorpion* (Ischnuridea hadogenes).

SNAKES ALIVE

Some of the more unfriendly snakes in Botswana include:
● **Egyptian cobra** – mainly in north and east of Botswana; up to 2m (6½ft) in length.
● **Mozambique spitting cobra** – up to 1.5m (5ft) long; nocturnal; found mainly in the Okavango and eastern regions of Botswana.
● **Black mamba** – fearsome, fast and aggressive; up to 2.5m (8ft) long.
● **Puff adder** – widespread; responsible for over 60% of serious bites due to its habit of sunning itself in pathways, where it is stepped on.
● **Boomslang** – a tree snake; maximum length of 2m (6½ft). It occurs throughout most of Botswana.

THE BUSHMEN

The Bushmen, or 'San', are the original inhabitants of southern Africa and derive their name from the Bakgothu word meaning 'those who gather wild food'. While their hunter-gatherer way of life has been overrun by modern man, an accurate record of their history has been preserved through the remarkable rock paintings they have left behind. The Bushmen believe in a special conservationist relationship between mankind and the nature which sustains them. Their unusual language is characterized by unique 'click' consonants. These are explained in greater detail on page 119.

HISTORY IN BRIEF

Remains of Palaeolithic man have been discovered throughout southern Africa, pointing to habitation for at least the last million years, but the earliest modern inhabitants of Botswana were the **San** (Bushmen). They have lived an almost unchanged lifestyle in the country since the Middle Stone Age. Having avoided the onslaught of modern man by retreating deeper and deeper into the wastelands, these remarkable people have managed to maintain their individualistic hunter-gatherer existence until as recently as the early 1980s when the last wandering family groups were unwillingly brought into the 'civilized' world.

The San were a peace-loving people who lived in harmony with nature, but not so the more dominant, socially organized **Bantu tribes** that migrated into the subcontinent from the Congo Basin about 1500 years ago. The peaceful San were no match for these tribal groups – who came with their knowledge of pottery, cattle rearing and iron working – and they were quickly conquered, being assimilated as slaves or driven away completely.

The first socially stratified Bantu 'chiefdoms' with a distinct class structure emerged in Botswana a thousand years ago near Palapye and, by AD1200, a second greater power had developed, with its capital on **Mapungubwe Hill** at the confluence of the Shashe and Limpopo rivers in the present-day Mashatu Game Reserve area. This hilltop community was soon eclipsed by the **Great Zimbabwe Empire** which spread its domain over much of eastern Botswana.

Following centuries of tribal nomadism and the endless splitting and

Below: *The scattered thatched huts of a traditional village punctuate the flat Kalahari sandscape.*

reforming of groups of people, almost all the fertile land in southern Africa had been occupied by the early 19th century. As a result the people became competitive, vying for the natural wealth that the land had to offer. Social unrest, tribal tension and chaos, all heightened by the growing ivory and slave

trades, ushered in a particularly violent and destructive period in Botswana's history.

Above: *A traditional Zulu village in the time of Shaka and his Impis.*

The Difaqane Wars

The Difaqane was a devastating wave of tribal wars that swept across much of southern Africa including Botswana in the early 1800s. It started in 1816 in South Africa's KwaZulu-Natal province where a Zulu prince named **Shaka** seized the throne and initiated a series of expansionist wars to extend his powerbase.

This violent upheaval had a domino effect as Shaka's opponents, who fled north, in turn conquered other tribes, sparking off more wars. Untold lives were lost, lands were devastated and the survivors scattered, spreading out across the northern regions of the subcontinent. One of the most notable northern migrations as a result of this turmoil was **Mzilikazi's** odyssey across Botswana to Bulawayo in Zimbabwe where his tribe eventually settled, establishing themselves as the proud Ndebele who still live in that area today.

By 1836 when the Zulu empire was at its peak, 20,000 **Boer Voortrekkers** left the Cape heading north to escape British rule. They too displaced many people, adding to the already confused flood of humanity. Although this tragic Difaqane period lasted just 20 years, countless people died and as many as 100,000 refugees were driven into the arid northwest.

MZILIKAZI'S ROUTE

In 1822 Mzilikazi, the Zulu king of the Amakhumalo clan, disagreed with Shaka over the ownership of some cattle. As a result he had to flee northwards with 300 of his people. But he was a strong leader and gathered many followers along the way. He eventually settled in the Magaliesburg Mountains where he began building the Amandebele Nation, and by 1830 he controlled all the land between the Vaal and Ngotwane rivers. In 1836 clashes with the Voortrekkers forced him to flee into Botswana, driving the Batswana away before him. In 1840, after four years moving through the country, Mzilikazi and his tribe settled in Bulawayo, leaving the Batswana to return and rebuild their communities.

THE JAMESON RAID

In an effort to stem the growing strength of the Boers in the Transvaal, Rhodes hoped to engineer an *Uitlanders* uprising in the province. To instigate this he planned an invasion led by one of his administrators, a Dr Jameson from Pitsanaphotlokwe within Botswana. It is believed that the plans were made in the Gaborone's Fort, the remains of which can still be seen in the residential area east of the Riverwalk shopping centre. This ill-fated raid, that ultimately led to the Anglo-Boer War, was launched on the night of 29 December 1895. It resulted in a humiliating surrender to the Boers on 2 January 1896. Britain was embarrassed and consequently reversed their decision to transfer the Bechuanaland Protectorate to Rhodes.

Missionaries and Merchants

The London Missionary Society (LMS) was formed in 1795 and by 1808 their first representative, Mr W. Edwards, had reached Kanye, but it was not until Moffat set up a permanent mission station at Kuruman in 1821 that Christianity began to spread into Botswana. Much of this was carried by the explorers and traders who wanted to open up the lucrative ivory routes. In 1841 David Livingstone arrived at Kuruman and, within a year, had visited the Bakwena. In 1845 after marrying Moffat's daughter Mary he settled among the Bakwena at Kolobeng where he established the first mission and school in the country; it was from this base that he organized his many trips into the African interior.

Ivory was to become Botswana's most sought after commodity and, although an elephant tusk would fetch just over one shilling, there was enough to bring great wealth to the tribes of central Botswana who bought guns to consolidate their power and unite their kingdoms. But even with this firepower they could not stem the growing tide of European traders and settlers who were spearheading the scramble for Africa.

In 1866, **gold** was discovered near Francistown and Africa's first gold rush ensued followed by another a few years later in Zimbabwe, where numerous other richer goldfields were discovered.

The Threat of Incorporation

The combined problems of colonial pressure and the Boer threat greatly worried the Tswana kings. **Cecil John Rhodes** was also concerned about the Boers and, in an effort to thwart their encroachment, in March 1885 he persuaded the British government to declare Botswana the 'British Protectorate of Bechuanaland.' This saved the country from the Boers, but strengthened Rhodes and his expansionist aspirations to incorporate Bechuanaland into Rhodesia (now Zimbabwe). The people of Botswana were left with the same problem, just a different adversary.

In order to solve this growing dilemma, in 1895, in a daring political move, three Tswana kings, **Khama**, **Bathoen** and **Sebele**, went to England to appeal to the British government not to transfer the Protectorate to Rhodes and his British South Africa Company. While the kings did receive the support of certain antislavery and humanitarian groups, it was only the failed **Jameson Raid** in the last days of 1895 that won them the support of the British government and secured the country's future as a Protectorate, with nominal involvement and interference.

There was a further threat to Bechuanaland's sovereignty in 1910 when the Union of South Africa attempted to incorporate the country, but the vigilant Tswana kings again successfully lobbied for exclusion. The protectorate status was to remain until full independence in 1966 and brought with it a long period of 'peaceful neglect', characterized by little development, but also with few of the colonial impositions suffered by every other country in southern and central Africa.

The Controversial Khama Marriage
It is sad to think that the most well-known episode in Botswana's history was the international campaign to ruin the marriage of Seretse and Ruth Khama.

Seretse Khama, the Prince Regent of the Bangwato, met **Ruth Williams** soon after World War II while he was studying law in London. They fell in love and Seretse announced his intention to marry the Englishwoman. Khama's uncle Tshekedi opposed this as it was the Ngwato tradition that a chief's wife should be a Motswana woman chosen by the tribal leaders.

Above: *Botswana's national flag, a symbol of unity and peace in southern Africa.*
Opposite: *Dr David Livingstone, the famous missionary and explorer who brought Christianity to Botswana and much of central Africa.*

THE NATIONAL FLAG

Unlike many other African flags with stripes of black and red reflecting the wars of liberation, Botswana's national flag is dominated by a tranquil blue. This is an intentional reflection of the peaceful, calm nature of the people, with the black and white stripes a symbol of racial harmony. The blue represents water and rain, which create prosperity. The black represents the black Batswana and the white represents the white Batswana, so together the flag conveys the ideal of a prosperous multiracial society living together in harmony.

Above: *The village* kgotla *or meeting place.*
Opposite: *Seretse Khama, Botswana's first president.*

VILLAGE DEMOCRACY

There has always been a democratic tradition among the Batswana in the form of the **kgotla**, or tribal court. This is a place where the common people and their leaders meet to discuss matters of importance and pass judgements. Here all people, regardless of social standing, have a chance to resolve problems. The *kgotla* is usually in the middle of the village under a tree outside the chief's residence. In modern Botswana the village *kgotla* is still the focal point of the community. If you are passing through tribal land and wish to ask permission to camp, or even if you are just seeking the services of a guide, start at the *kgotla* and respectfully ask if you can speak to the **kgosi** (chief). His endorsement will ensure the help of everyone.

The British were also strongly against the marriage, which took place on 29 September 1948. Apart from their own prejudices, they feared that it would offend the administrations in Rhodesia and particularly South Africa with whom the British were anxious to negotiate a plutonium deal. To separate the couple, Seretse was enticed to England on an official invitation and then refused re-entry into his own country.

Soon afterwards Ruth joined Seretse in London where they lived together in exile for five years before being permitted back home in 1956, after Seretse and his children had renounced their claim to chieftainship. But this renunciation left Seretse free to pursue a successful political career.

Soon after his triumphant return he became actively involved in the formation of the Botswana Democratic Party (BDP) and the drive towards independence, as a result of which he was destined to become the first president of Botswana and eventually to be knighted by the Queen of England.

Independence
Indicative of the lack of interest shown in the Bechuanaland Protectorate by the British, the colony was administered from **Mafikeng** in South Africa, making it one of the few countries in the world to have had its capital outside its national boundaries.

Sir Charles Rey, the Commissioner of the Protectorate in the early 1930s, worked vigorously for greater development of the country and was the first advocate for moving the country's capital to within its borders. But this was not to happen until independence some 30 years later.

HISTORICAL CALENDAR

25,000BC–AD1000 San occupy Botswana leaving artefacts and rock paintings.
1000 Bantu peoples move in, displacing the San.
1100 First hilltop chiefdoms.
1200 Mapungubwe Hill becomes the most important political centre in the country.
1400 The Bakgalagadi settle in western Transvaal and eastern Botswana.
1500 Batswana migrate westward into Botswana.
1750 The Batswana occupy fertile land in Botswana.
1816 Shaka seizes Zulu throne.
1820 Difaqane Wars begin.
1830 Mzilikazi betrays Shaka and flees northwest, attacking the Batswana.
1837 The Voortrekkers drive Mzilikazi into Botswana.
1840 Mzilikazi and his people move to Bulawayo.

1841 David Livingstone is the first Christian missionary to enter Botswana.
1848 Sechele the Paramount Chief of the Bakwena is converted to Christianity.
1866 Gold discovered at Tati.
1872 Khama III installed as Chief of the Ngwato.
1885 British extend Protectorate status to Bechuanaland.
1895 Khama, Bathoen and Sebele visit England to stop the transfer of the Protectorate to Rhodes.
1896 The Jameson Raid fails.
1921 Seretse Khama born.
1923 Khama III dies 23 Feb.
1948 Seretse Khama marries Ruth Williams.
1950 The multi-racial 'Joint Advisory Council' established.
1956 The Khama family returns from exile.
1962 The Botswana Democratic Party is formed

with Seretse Khama as its leader.
1963 Construction of the capital city Gaborone begins.
1966 Botswana gains full independence, Sir Seretse Khama installed as the first president.
1967 Diamonds found at Orapa.
1980 Sir Seretse Khama dies.
1991 President Dr Ketumile Masire is knighted by Queen Elizabeth II.
1998 Botswana established as first International Financial Services Center on mainland Africa. Masire steps down and Festus Mogae becomes Botswana's third President.
2000 Sedudu Island is confirmed as part of Botswana by the International Court in the Hague.

In the early 1960s Gaborone was selected as the site of the new capital and frenetic construction began immediately. In 1965 the Bechuanaland Protectorate was granted internal self-government as a prequel to the birth of the Republic of Botswana and full independence on 30 September 1966, under the leadership of Seretse Khama.

Sir Seretse Khama died in 1980, a highly respected leader and politician, and was succeeded by the vice president, **Dr Ketumile Masire**, who continued the Botswana Democratic Party's drive towards a free, democratic and capitalist society.

Having achieved excellent economic growth, prosperity and political stability through the '70s, '80s and '90s, when many of her neighbours were ravaged by violence and

THE HERALDIC STANDARD

The central element in Botswana's coat of arms is a shield containing three inter-locking **cogs**, which represent industrial progress in all sectors; three **waves** which represent water implying prosperity and peace; and the **head of a cow**, being the traditional symbol of wealth. The shield is supported by two **zebras**, the national animal. One zebra holds a stalk of corn and the other an ele-phant tusk, symbolizing the important balance between the country's natural resources and agricultural activities. Beneath the coat of arms is a scroll with the word **Pula**. Pula is the Setswana word for rain, which brings prosperity, goodwill and peace.

Below: *The massive Haulpak trucks that work in Jwaneng diamond mine's open-cast pit are some of the largest trucks in the world.*

war, Botswana now looks forward to continued prosper-ity as much of southern Africa can at last enjoy peaceful coexistence and international investment.

GOVERNMENT AND ECONOMY

Since independence the **Botswana Democratic Party** (BDP) has governed the country. The British system of parliamentary rule and democracy was inherited by the Botswana government and, under the inspired leader-ship of Seretse Khama, Botswana was one of the few countries in Africa to choose democracy over socialism at independence.

The head of state is the president who is elected to serve a term of five years by the 34-member National Assembly of Parliament which holds legislative powers and includes the 15 cabinet ministers. The House of Chiefs is made up of 15 chiefs and tribal representa-tives whose function is to advise the National Assembly on proposed laws relating to land usage as well as social and traditional customs.

Botswana is divided into nine 'districts' each administered separately by a District Commissioner who is responsible for the implementation of the gov-ernment's various development programmes. Time has proven the failings of socialism and, while many of Botswana's neighbours are restructuring their political and economic systems, Botswana is reaping the bene-fits of a free-market, capitalist economic policy.

Batswana society is based on a concept of social harmony, which in Setswana is called *kagisano*. This enshrines the ideals of unity, peace, harmony and a sense of community. In the modern political context, *kagisano* still forms an im-portant part of the country's National Development Plan, by determining the four national principles of *Ditiro tsa ditl-*

habololo (Development), *Boipelego* (Self-reliance), *Popagao ya sechaba* (Unity) and *Puso ya batho ka batho* (Democracy), which are all derived from Batswana culture.

Rather like capitalism, the concept of democracy being enshrined as a national pillar is quite unique in Africa. There has always been an established and active opposition in Botswana's political arena, and the regular elections are contested by a diverse range of parties.

While there are regular cries of foul play and accusations of corruption, the political environment in Botswana is remarkably stable with an adherence to non-violent political negotiation, and *kgotla*-style dialogue.

A Diamond-studded Economy

The degree of Botswana's success is reflected in the fact that for the first twenty years since independence Botswana enjoyed the highest growth rate of GNP per capita in the world.

The reason for this phenomenal growth was the comparative lack of development at independence in 1966 and the discovery of diamonds in 1967. **De Beers** had been prospecting in the country for 12 years prior to this discovery, but even they were not prepared for the significance of the massive diamond reserves in Botswana.

By value, Botswana is the largest diamond producer in the world with an annual output of about 20 million carats, in some years accounting for up to 30% of De Beers' Central Selling Organization's (CSO) total sale. This is significant when one appreciates that the CSO distributes over 80% of the world's total production.

Orapa Diamond Mine went into full production in 1971 following the construction of the mine, the town and a new road network. By 1977, when **Letlhekane Mine** started production, Orapa had become one of the largest diamond mines in the world, but then **Jwaneng** was discovered. Opened in 1982, it is now one of the richest diamond mines in the world.

Above: *Sorting diamonds, the mainstay of Botswana's burgeoning economy.*

A Beacon of Hope

In 1972, the President, Sir Seretse Khama, said 'Botswana is widely regarded as a beacon of hope in a troubled region, and a force for constructive change. We as a nation, should be an example in the defence and development of non-racialism and social justice for all.' Sir Seretse Khama worked relentlessly at setting this example for other nations to follow and Botswana has indeed remained a shining example of a harmonious non-racial society in a troubled continent.

Above: *Elephant-back safaris offer an exciting and unique way of see the Okavango Delta.*

Since independence, diamonds have accounted for approximately 75% of Botswana's total export earnings and just under half of the country's gross domestic product. With diamonds as the single major driving force, the government has been actively attempting to diversify the economy, but while there is evidence of considerable mineral wealth, including possible natural gas and oil deposits, most other mining ventures have not achieved full potential.

In 2003 the discovery of new gold deposits east of Francistown breathed new life into the country's almost completely mothballed gold-mining industry. The only other large scale mining operation in Botswana is the massive soda ash project on Sowa Pan, which, since it began operating in the early 1990s, has had to face numerous challenges from plummeting world prices to devastating flooding of the pan.

Wildlife and Tourism

Tourism is a significant foreign exchange earner for Botswana with estimated annual earnings being in excess of US$ 80 million. In the past, hunting trophy fees were the main contributor to this industry, but during the 1980s the emphasis began to change to photographic and ecotourism operations.

Although tourism already provides 40% of formal employment in the north of the country, it is still a major growth industry, and with the government's continual development of land usage plans and new area allocations, opportunities are always becoming available for tourism entrepreneurs. Scores of operators in Botswana offer anything from self-drive or guided safari vehicle hire to elephant-back safaris, but to preserve the country's pristine environment the government's stated policy of low-volume, high-cost tourism remains. Thus, while Botswana may be more expensive than Kenya or other high-volume safari destinations, it is still an exclusive unspoiled destination which, through care and official policy, is likely to remain so.

The Department of Wildlife and National Parks, which administers all of the national parks and conservation areas in Botswana, sets various conditions which visitors must abide by when entering any national park. These cover standard rules for human safety and others for the safety of the animals. But as conditions change and tourist pressure increases, the rules are often amended and new ones are added. For example, in 1996 it became necessary to pre-book any overnight visit to Botswana's northern game reserves through the Reservations Office in Maun (tel: 686-1265, fax: 686-1264, P.O. Box 20364, Boseja, Maun) and consequently any visitors arriving at the park gates without a booking will not be permitted entry. The office is open every day and bookings can be made up to 12 months in advance.

CITES BAN

With the international ban on the trade of elephant products Botswana's ivory income has been halted, but with the over-population of elephants in the Chobe the country could generate revenue from the sale and relocation of live elephants to private reserves. Unfortunately, the distance from northern Botswana makes this prohibitive which, combined with the ban on hunting (due to CITES), means that the government has had to consider elephant culling to stabilize the population and protect the environment from further and permanent damage.

Below: *A commercial cattle rancher inspecting his free-range herd.*

Ranching and Agriculture

With persistent drought and soaring summer temperatures, only 0.61% of Botswana is considered to be arable land with 0.02% of the country used for permanent crops of which less than 20km^2 (9 square miles) is under irrigation. Yet almost the entire rural population is involved in either subsistence farming of maize and sorghum or livestock rearing.

Above: *Mechanized commercial agriculture is limited to the southeastern corridor of Botswana.*

There are a few commercial farms in the Tuli Block as well as tracts of cultivated land around Gaborone, Pandamatenga and Kasane where a variety of crops and fruit is grown. Production is limited, however, and while certain food products such as pasta are exported to South Africa, the country still imports the majority of its food.

Cattle ranching is much more successful, with vast areas producing excellent free-range beef. As a revenue earner the industry has always been second only to mining, but with the problem of lung disease in Ngamiland in the 1990s and the diversification of the economy, manufacturing and financial services have surpassed the beef industry. However, cattle are still a symbol of wealth in traditional Batswana society where a man's social standing is reflected in the size of his herd. Even with the huge lung disease culls of 1996, cattle still outnumber people in Botswana by at least 2 to 1. This volume of cattle is, however, resulting in widespread overgrazing of the fragile grasslands.

The **Botswana Meat Commission** handles all beef exports from Botswana, the quality of which is world renowned. For much of the 1980s and '90s the country benefited from a preferential trade agreement to supply a quota of beef to the European Community. In Lobatse, where the beef industry is based, there is also a canning factory and a tannery which supplies top quality leather to, amongst others, the Italian shoe and fashion industries.

Manufacturing

To reduce its reliance on the fluctuating diamond market and to increase employment of Batswana, the government has tried to encourage investment in the manufacturing industry. These measures have included tax holidays, financial assistance and even across-the-board tax reductions. They have achieved a degree of success, with the manufacturing sector growing at an average rate of over 20% per annum between 1965 and 1985, faster than virtually any other country in the world, including Singapore and Indonesia.

Locally manufactured goods include textiles, metal products, plastics, electrical products, chemicals, vaccines, soap, shoes, building materials, food and drink. In addition there are several vehicle assembly plants which supply trucks, busses and cars to the local market.

THE PEOPLE

Almost two million people from numerous tribes and backgrounds live in Botswana, but despite this diversity, remarkable unity has been achieved as almost everyone considers themselves to be Batswana first, and tribespeople second.

The largest tribal group in Botswana is the original **Tswana** tribe, which still comprises almost 50% of the entire population, followed by the **Bakalanga** people who occupy the northeast and central districts of Botswana where they have lived for almost 1000 years.

The riverine tribes of the **Bayei**, **Basubiya** and **Hambu-kushu** inhabit the Okavango and Chobe waterways in Ngamiland District, subsisting on the water and its rich natural resources. The

---

DISEASE CONTROL

In 1896 rinderpest killed hundreds of thousands of animals in Botswana including both cattle and wildlife. This lead to the establishment of the Veterinary Department in 1905, but it was only after the outbreak of foot-and-mouth disease in the late 1970s that the Botswana Vaccine Institute was established to control and eradicate the disease. With the development of the beef industry and access to the European markets through the Lomé agreement, Botswana set up thousands of kilometres of cordon fences to separate cattle from the disease-carrying buffalo. These strict, often unpopular measures have protected the national herd from foot-and-mouth disease, but tragically, in 1996, there was an outbreak of lung disease in Ngamiland, and hundreds of thousands of cattle in northern Botswana had to be destroyed.

Below: *Herero women in their beautiful, but impractical, traditional dresses.*

Bayei were the first to arrive in the 1700s, closely followed by the Basubiya who established their capital at Luchindo on the Chobe River. The Hambukushu are master basket weavers who are recent additions to the cultural tapestry of Botswana. They arrived in waves from Namibia and Angola over the past couple of hundred years,

Above: *A San family works at traditional crafts.*

with the last group of 4000 moving into the country in 1969 to escape the Angolan civil war.

The **Bakgalagadi** tribe are also of Sotho-Tswana origin and are closely related to the Batswana people, sharing similar customs and beliefs. Many Bakgalagadi still practise subsistence agriculture and often occupy the 'Remote Area Dweller' category.

The **San** are also deep rural dwellers who shy away from contact with the larger villages with which they are unfamiliar. However, now that they are no longer able to pursue their traditional hunter-gatherer lifestyles, they rely on government assistance programmes.

The Changing Lifestyle of the San

There is a common misconception that the San are on the verge of extinction with just a few isolated family groups wandering the Central Kalahari. On the contrary, Botswana has a growing San population of up to 60,000 but their hunter-gatherer way of life is now extinct and they are reeling from tremendous social and cultural change. These changes have deprived the San of their cultural independence and have destroyed their social structure, leaving many of them in extreme poverty, dependent on an undignified existence of government handouts and vulnerable to exploitation and racial prejudice.

SOUTHWARD MIGRATION

The Bantu-speaking people of southern Africa are believed to have originated from the central rainforests of Gabon and Cameroon about 2500 years ago when there was a rapid population explosion and the tribes began to migrate. First they moved towards the Great Lakes of central Africa and then turned southwards, arriving in Zimbabwe and the east coast of South Africa in about AD200, bringing with them cattle, small stock and the knowledge of both pottery and iron-working. Within several hundred years these people had come to dominate the subcontinent, which had been well populated with a rich tribal tapestry and a widespread network of chiefdoms.

In addition to these various tribes, there is a significant group of white Batswana, comprised of descendants of the original missionaries, farmers and traders who have permanently settled in the country over the last 100 years.

The Tswana

Essentially pastoralists for whom cattle are extremely important, the Tswana people who form the majority of the country's population have given their tribal name, with the plural prefix 'Ba' to describe the people of Botswana – hence the term 'Batswana'. In Botswana there are three major groups of Tswana people: the Bakwena who live in the Molepolole area, the Bangwaketse who live in the Kanye area, and the Bangwato who live in the Palapye and Serowe areas and to whom the Khama family belongs.

The Traditional Dress of the Herero

The Herero originated in Namibia and only recently moved into the north of the country around Lake Ngami in 1904–1905 to escape the Germans.

The remarkable traditional dresses that Herero woman wear are the result of a German missionary's zealous wife Mrs Emma Hahn, who – 150 years ago – wanted to eliminate nudity amongst Herero women, so taught them to sew. The Herero women copied the Victorian-style dresses that the missionary wives wore, making their own adaptations, including the bright colours and the two-pointed headdress, which represents a young cow's horns.

Herero women still sew these dresses, using up to 10m (33ft) of fabric to make the pleated skirt, and reams of material to make the numerous petticoats. The outfits are heavy and impractical, especially in summer, but one will often see women in

---

A TOLERANT PEOPLE

Having been spared the full effects of colonial rule, and with a tradition of providing refuge for any displaced people, Batswana are well known for their relaxed, welcoming attitude and their remarkable racial and tribal tolerance. Over the last 100 years this has made Botswana one of the most peaceful countries on the African continent. As a result Botswana has also been spared the ravages of civil wars and liberation struggles that have marred the history of all her neighbours.

Below: *A San hunter uses his traditional light bow and poisoned arrows, coupled with his incredible stealth and tracking skills.*

SPEAK THE LANGUAGE

These phrases might come in handy when conversing with the local peoples:

Hello sir/madam •
Dumela Rra/Mma
Hello gentlemen/ladies •
Dumelang borra/bomma
How are you? • *O kae?*
I am fine • *Ke teng*
Stay well (said when you're leaving) • *Sala sentle*
Travel well (said when someone else is leaving) •
Tsamaya sentle
Sleep well • *Robala sentle*
Thank you • *Ke itumetse/tanki*
Okay/fine/yes • *Go siame*
No • *Nnyaa*
Petrol • *Lookwae/Peterolo*
Bread • *Borotho/Senkgwe*
Water • *Metsi*
I want to see the doctor •
Ke batla go bona ngaka
How much does this cost? • *Ke bokae?*

their traditional dress, especially in Maun. However, remember that if you want to take photographs of Herero women in traditional dress, it is important to ask permission first and a small fee is usually charged.

Language

Setswana is the national language and all the major tribes speak it with minor differences in dialect. This contributes to their tribal harmony. However, English is the official business language and it is widely spoken in the urban areas with most written communication being in this language. In certain rural areas and smaller commercial centres Afrikaans is often used. This is as a result of the significant number of Batswana who were employed as migrant labour on the mines in South Africa.

Religion

While **Christianity** is now the official religion in Botswana, and certainly the strongest, with well over 60% of the population abiding by its tenets, a variety of different faiths are also practised. Certain traditional beliefs have been incorporated into modern Christianity, such as the concept of *Modimo*, the supreme being. The

Zion Christian Church is the strongest denomination, and its followers can be identified by the small felt-backed silver star that they wear.

Christianity was brought into Botswana by **David Livingstone** in the middle of the 19th century and **Sechele I**, the Chief of the Bakwena was the first Motswana to be converted to Christianity. This conversion was probably more as a result of shrewd political – rather than spiritual – motivation in an attempt to secure British support and approval, as at his conversion the chief remarked to Livingstone, 'If you like I shall call my headmen and, with our whips, we shall soon make them all believe.'

There is a strong **Muslim** community in Botswana, while in Gaborone North there is a **Buddhist** Meditation Centre where there grows a seedling of the original 'Bo' fig tree (*Ficus religiosa*), under which Prince Siddhartha, the founder of Buddhism, gained 'enlightenment' or *bodhi* some 2500 years ago.

Food and Drink

Wholesome traditional food is available in most restaurants throughout Botswana and for foreign visitors it is well worth a try, even though some of it, such as dried **mopane worms** (highly nutritious with an appealing nutty flavour) may require an open mind and a strong will. **Seswaa** is the traditional beef dish and is served with *pap*, which is a soft maize meal.

Traditional **beer** is also very popular – and potent – usually being served from a large clay pot into hollow gourds. Unlike western beers it is not clear, but has a distinct texture. *Chibuku* is the commercially brewed version of this beer and, although very low in alcohol, is interesting for its unfamiliar lumpy consistency. In a calculated government policy to protect the income of many otherwise unemployed women, this cardboard-cartonned drink is not available in official liquor stores, and can only be bought from the *shebeens*. Ask your local guide where you can buy some as it is definitely worth a taste.

In Ngamiland around the Okavango and Makgadikgadi areas, where the real fan palm (*Hyphaene petersiana*) and wild date palms (*Phoenix reclinata*) are common, a very intoxicating **palm wine** known locally as *muchema* is distilled from their sap. Unfortunately, this is not easily found as the tapping process often leads to the death of the trees, which are also under threat from the commercial basket weavers who reap the new leaves of these palms to make their wares.

Above: *For the gourmet with a strong constitution, the mopane worm offers an interesting alternative to everyday fare.*
Opposite: *The imposing, buttressed London Missionary Society church in Serowe.*

CULTURAL AWARENESS

In Botswana you'll notice many interesting customs, such as the way people hand things to each other with one hand grasping the other wrist to show they are not concealing a weapon behind their back. You may also be surprised by the way men push in front of women through doors and lifts. Unlike in Western culture, in traditional Batswana society men always go through doors first to ward off impending danger on the other side. So remember if a man pushes in front of you, it might not be because he's being disrespectful!

2
Gaborone and Surrounds

As one of Africa's fastest growing cities, **Gaborone**, Botswana's capital, is a vibrant, colourful metropolis. Due to its phenomenal growth from an obscure village in the early 1960s to home to more than 230,000 people in just 40 years, Gaborone has neither a long history nor an established traditional African character, as certain other African cities such as Dar es Salaam and Nairobi do. Gaborone does, however, still provide all the facilities you would expect to find in any modern city.

The tiny administrative village of Gaberone's (literally 'Gaberone's place') was selected in 1964 as the site of the country's new capital primarily because of its reliable water supply, its strategic location and its proximity to the '**Cape to Cairo**' railway line.

The city is named after **Chief Gaberone** who lead the Batlokwa tribe into the area in the 1880s. They settled in Tlokweng, the first urban area you reach when driving into the city from the South African border post 20km (12 miles) to the east. In the early 1890s a colonial fort was built in an area now known as The Village near Tlokweng, and its ruins can still be seen near the Village Health Club.

The unsuccessful **Jameson Raid** in 1895 that sparked off the Anglo-Boer War was planned by Cecil John Rhodes in Gaborone at a time when there was little more than a handful of buildings in the area.

When Botswana gained independence from Britain on 30 September 1966, Gaborone had just the administrative essentials and a mere 1000 new homes. Two years later it was declared a city and has continued to grow ever since.

DON'T MISS

★★★ Mokolodi Game Reserve: take a walk with the elephants.
★★★ Tracking rhino through the Mokolodi Hills.
★★ A climb up **Kgale Hill.**
★★ Gaborone Game Reserve: for a barbecue breakfast.
★★ Gaborone Dam: perfect for fishing or picnicking.
★★ National Museum and Art Gallery: Botswana baskets and other exhibitions.
★ President Hotel's 'Terrace': enjoy tea while overlooking the main shopping Mall.

Opposite: *A regal Seretse Khama in front of the parliament buildings.*

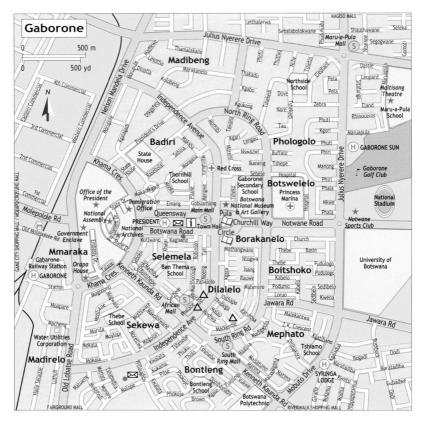

Gaborone

0   500 m
0   500 yd

N

GABORONE

Gaborone is generally the point of entry into Botswana, through the bustling Sir Seretse Khama International Airport or through its road links with South Africa, providing access for tourists to the main attractions of the Okavango Delta, the Chobe, Tuli Block and the more remote desert areas.

Built around an original circular layout, Gaborone has since experienced frenetic growth. This can be appreciated in the disjointed and confusing layout of the city's roads and suburbs.

Opposite: *Vendors and craftsmen display their wares under the shady trees of Gaborone's paved central Mall.*

The city offers a range of modern hotels, casinos, cinemas, a choice of good restaurants, and night clubs, many of which host live performances by the popular artists of Botswana's burgeoning music industry. Well-patronized venues include the Bull & Bush just off Nelson Mandela Drive, and the Take 5 Club in Mogoditshane 4km (2.5 miles) northeast of Gaborone.

A Shopping Paradise ★★

With its rapid growth and the greater priority for the administrative essentials, Gaborone has never had a reputation as a great place to shop. But as a result of the growing national prosperity and urban disposable income, this has changed over the last few years and now Gaborone has more retail shopping space per person than almost any other city in the world. Of course this over-expansion has come with its own problems, but for the visitor there is an amazing choice of modern shopping malls, all laced with trendy restaurants and coffee shops, each vying for the shopper's attention with top quality imported and local products. 'Must visit' malls in Gaborone include the massive **Game City** at the base of Kgale Hill, **Riverwalk Shopping Mall** on the north bank of the Ngotwane River, **Molapo Crossing**, **Fairground Mall**, **Broadhurst** (especially for the Saturday market), and the old **Main Mall**.

The National Assembly ★★

The National Assembly is at the top of the main Mall where it is surrounded by the other tall government buildings. At the centre of this government enclave is a paved square with a War Memorial for those Batswana who gave their lives for the British Empire, and a statue of Sir Seretse Khama, Botswana's first president.

Above: *In the grounds of the National Museum, off Gaborone's busy Independence Avenue, a traditional Batswana hut provides a 'live exhibit' for visitors.*

On the other side of the Mall there is a good **public library** next to the Town Hall. It boasts a wide selection of books covering all aspects of Botswana's history, people and culture, as does the **British Council** opposite Debswana House. The library is open on Monday 13:00–17:30, Tuesday–Friday 10:00–17:30, Saturday 09:00–12:00 .

National Sports Centre ★

The impressive national sports centre, built in the 1980s, is just 2km (1½ miles) east of the main Mall on Nyerere Drive between the Gaborone Golf Club and the University of Botswana. League football matches are played here most weekends in addition to other sporting and cultural events. Next to the stadium are the Botswana Tennis Association courts, which have hosted the international Davis Cup competition; the Cricket Club grounds and clubhouse; and the Squash Club courts. All the courts are open to the public daily, although tennis and squash courts can generally only be booked by club members.

National Museum and Art Gallery ★★★

Gaborone houses the National Museum and Art Gallery, which displays a collection of traditional crafts and paintings by local and regional artists and has original works by **Thomas Baines**. The Botswana Society have their offices at the museum and if you are interested in the country's history, these are worth a visit. Open Tuesday–Friday 09:00–18:00; weekends and public holidays 09:00–17:00.

Another gallery is **Gallery Ann**, a small private art gallery and framing shop in the Craft Workshop shopping centre off Nakedi Road in Broadhurst. Open Monday–Friday 09:00–17:00, Saturday 09:00–13:00.

CRAFT MARKETS

★★★ Lentswe-la-Oodi Weavers in Oodi village about 20km (12 miles) from Gaborone on the Francistown road. Tour the factory and buy colourful ethnic wall hangings and tapestries.
★★ Botswana Craft, on the Western Bypass towards the airport traffic circle, specializes in southern African curios and Botswana baskets.
★ Informal street market under the shady trees of the main Mall.
★ The Borakanelo Flea Market every Sunday in the BBS Mall, Broadhurst Shopping Centre.

Theatres ★★

There are several established performing arts venues, the main one being the **Maitisong Cultural Centre**. Maitisong is at Maru-a-Pula school, and hosts the **National Maitisong Festival** in March as well as numerous performances organized by various groups. There is also a very active local drama group called **Capital Players**. Details of these and other performances by numerous traditional dance and drama groups can be found in the weekly *Advertiser*.

Gaborone Game Reserve ★★★

This 550ha (1359 acre) reserve was opened in 1988 through the efforts of the Kalahari Conservation Society, and is now Botswana's third-busiest reserve. It provides an ideal getaway for those wanting to escape the stresses of urban life.

There is a small entrance fee and visitors can see a remarkable range of wildlife including one or two rhino, eland, kudu and red hartebeest. A detailed route map is supplied at the entrance gate, a short distance off Limpopo Drive on the western side of the city.

Bird watching in the Gaborone Game Reserve is excellent, particularly along the eastern edge bounded by the Ngotwane River. There are two well-maintained picnic sites and a game hide. Open daily 06:30–18:30.

Mokolodi Game Reserve ★★★

Opened in mid-1994 this 3000ha (7380 acre) reserve was established by the Mokolodi Wildlife Foundation and, as well as managing the game reserve, the Foundation runs Botswana's first and only Environmental Education Centre teaching children the importance of conserving the wealth of wildlife and natural resources that their country has to offer.

Set in a wide valley between the **Mokolodi Hills** and 'Magic Mountain' – inhabited by leopard and porcupine –

THE RHINO LEGACY

White or 'square-lipped' rhinos have been reintroduced into the Mokolodi Game Reserve, but generations ago these massive prehistoric creatures, reputed to be the largest pure grazers to have ever walked the earth, were common in the Gaborone area. In the Mokolodi Game Reserve near permanent water holes are a couple of ancient 'rhino rubbing stones' polished smooth by many centuries of use. Now that these creatures have been reintroduced these stones and certain trees at their favourite mudholes are again being rubbed smooth by the huge abrasive bulks of these endangered creatures.

Below: *A full-grown white rhinoceros (Ceratotherium simum), although less aggressive than the black rhino, still weighs in at over 2000kg (4400lb).*

this scenic reserve has a well-developed network of game viewing drives. The roads can be a bit rough in places, but most are negotiable in two-wheel-drive vehicles. Naturally occurring game includes kudu, impala, brown hyena, water buck and leopard; while rhino, mountain reedbuck, zebra, hartebeest, sable, giraffe, gemsbok, and tame cheetah and elephant have been introduced.

Over the weekends Mokolodi offers numerous guided **game drives**. The early morning and late evening drives are the most rewarding as during the heat of the day most animals retreat into the shade. The evening drives, which can incorporate a fantastic 'bush braai' dinner, are good for spotting the more unusual nocturnal creatures such as the small cats, porcupines and spring hares.

There are five **self-catering chalets** overlooking a water hole in the reserve for overnight visitors, plus a gift and curio shop, a bar and indigenous botanical garden. Access to these facilities is free, but there is an entrance fee for the reserve. Mokolodi can also arrange special transport to collect visitors from any of the hotels in Gaborone.

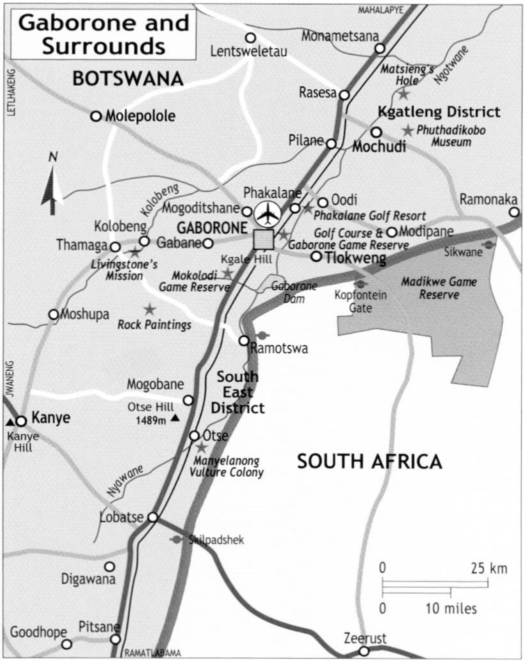

Gaborone Dam ★★★

As the only significant water supply in the area, Gaborone Dam was built in the early stages of the city's development. With the rapidly growing population and subsequent demand for more water, the dam wall was raised in the 1980s, greatly increasing the surface area of the dam and flooding the old Lobatse road.

Gaborone and Surrounds

BOTSWANA

SOUTH AFRICA

0   25 km

0   10 miles

Surrounded by high hills and thick game filled bush, the setting for 'Gabs Dam' is very attractive. There are plans for a 'Waterfront' leisure development on the edge of the dam, but currently there is only the 'City Scapes' picnic site on the east bank, a 'members only' clubhouse for the Kalahari Fishing Club and the Yacht Club which is set on a rocky island in the middle of the dam. There is a simple restaurant, bar, swimming pool and wide veranda overlooking the water.

Above: *The king of all the beasts,* Panthera leo *surveys his domain.*

There is also an enjoyable boat ride to the island (depending on the water level) and for a daily fee non-member visitors are very welcome.

One does, however, need a Water Ultilities **permit** to get to the water's edge. These can be purchased from the Corporations offices at Plot 17530, Luthuli Road. Gaborone Dam is a good fishing venue where **bass**, **bream** and **barbell** (catfish) can be caught.

The dam is also popular with birders for its wide range of **water birds** and **bee-eaters**. Be aware that there is a danger of bilharzia and crocodiles, so swimming in the dam should be avoided.

Kgale Hill **

Gaborone is dominated by Kgale Hill on the western edge of the city. It offers a pleasant climb with breath-taking views of the dam and city. Visitors can choose one of three well-defined routes up the hill: the steep **Rusty's Route** up the rocky face; the longer **Transfeldt Trail** up the back; and the undulating walk across the saddle to **Cross Kopje**. Each takes less than an hour.

There is a resident troop of baboons living on Kgale and a pair of black eagles consistently nests in the craggy cliff face just below the peak. There have also been reports of early morning sightings of leopard. But, before leaving your car at the base of the hill, it is worth hiring someone from Old Naledi to guard your vehicle as there have been instances of petty theft in the car park area.

THE BOER WAR

After the **Battle of Crocodile Pools** just outside Gaborone in 1899, the British police and officials stationed at Gaborone were ordered to retreat and destroy the administrative camp there. The only article left of value was a huge safe, but when the Boers who had overrun the area blew it open, all they found was a piece of paper with the words 'sold again!'
But not all the war history of Gaborone was so amusing. A bitter battle was fought in the Crocodile Pools area on the hills near Mokolodi overlooking the Metswemaswaane River. Heavy artillery was used by both sides, numerous soldiers were killed, a VC was awarded and the railway bridge over the river was blown up. Grave sites can still be found on the hill on the eastern side of the bridge.

MATSIENG'S FOOTPRINTS

This is one of the four known 'creation' sites in Botswana where, according to local legend, Matsieng (the 'Adam' of Batswana folklore) emerged from the muddy river bed followed by all the animals of the earth. An elongated human footprint and animal spoor engravings, estimated to be between 3000 and 10,000 years old, can be seen at this protected archaeological site. The turn-off to the site can be found on the Francistown road north of Mochudi, about 2km (1.2 miles) after the Rasesa signpost.

Opposite: *The donkey cart is a common form of transport throughout rural Botswana.*
Below: *Brightly coloured woven wall hangings from the Lentswe-la-Oodi Weavers depict traditional village scenes.*

ALONG THE FRANCISTOWN ROAD

There are a few traditional villages north of Gaborone on the Francistown road which are famous for their craft centres and well worth a visit.

Phakalane ★

From the airport traffic circle take the Francistown road for 8km (5 miles) to the Phakalane turn-off which is on the right. The main attraction here is the **Phakalane Golf Club**. It offers a beautifully designed international standard 18-hole golf course with a restaurant and bar at the Clubhouse as well as luxury accommodation and the 'Blue Tree' putting green.

On the edge of Phakalane on the Ruretse road are a series of old stilling ponds, protected as the most important wetland area in the whole of southern Botswana with a resident population of **flamingoes**, **ducks** and unusual water birds including **avocets** and **gallinules**.

Oodi ★★

The first village along the Francistown road is Oodi, signposted about 3km (2 miles) beyond Phakalane. The village is about 5km (3 miles) off the main road set under the imposing Oodi Hill. The main attraction here are the **Lentswe-la-Oodi Weavers**, renowned for their ethnic wall hangings and tapestries. Visitors are welcome and during working hours the artists can be seen weaving their colourful creations.

Mochudi ★★

Another 10km (6 miles) along the road is the sprawling traditional village of Mochudi. Here, tourists will find examples of decorated **Setswana architecture**, the most southerly **baobabs** in Botswana, and **traditional crafts** including the **Ithukeng Tin Workshop** and **Ikabiseng handmade jewellery**.

Mochudi also has the only traditional working forge in Botswana, where a blacksmith can be seen practising his centuries-old craft under the sponsorship of Skillshare Africa, an organization dedicated to preserving the dying crafts and skills of Africa.

The **Phuthadikobo Museum** in Mochudi is also well worth a visit with exhibits focusing on the Kgatleng District and the Bakgatla people who have lived in the area since 1871. The museum overlooks the village from its cliff-top location. To get to it, park at the *kgotla* at the base of the hill and follow a well-maintained path up the incline. Open weekdays 08:00–17:00, weekends 14:00–17:00.

WEST OF GABORONE

The villages to the west of Gaborone are set in scenic, hilly country and are rich in crafts and history.

Kolobeng ★★

The Kanye road crosses the Kolobeng River 40km (25 miles) from Gaborone. Immediately after the bridge, on the left, is a short dirt road to the **Livingstone Memorial** and the ruins of David Livingstone's house and mission, built in the 1840s. The **church,** the first in Botswana, was where Chief Sechele was converted to Christianity. It was also the first school and the site of the first irrigation project. The foundations of these buildings can still be seen, as can the graves of Livingstone's daughter and the artist Thomas Dolman, both buried on the banks of the river.

KGOSI SECHELE I MUSEUM

This museum in Molepolole records the history and the fast disappearing life and culture of the Kweneng region as well as the Bakwena 'Crocodile' people who live there. The museum offers visitors fascinating escorted full- or half-day tours to historical sites in the area for a very reasonable fee.

THE ALOE FOREST

Near the Scottish Livingstone Hospital in Molepolole is an officially protected forest of aloes. These tall and remarkably old trees are unique not only for their profusion but because local legend has it that they once saved Molepolole from attack! The story goes that one dark night back in 1850 a raiding party of Boers crept up on the village, but mistaking the aloes for a standing army of defenders they thought they were outnumbered and ran away. These aloes bloom with massive orange flowers in September/October just before the first rains.

Above: *The Thamaga Pottery shop has gained local fame for the high quality of its wares.*

LIVINGSTONE'S CAVES

Just 5km (3 miles) from Molepolole on the Thamaga road there is a noticable cliff face on the northern side of the road. About 50m (165ft) up the cliff is a cave, and it was this craggy crevice that helped bring Christianity to the country in the late 1840s. The Kwena witchdoctor said that anyone who entered the cave would die, and it is believed that Chief Sechele converted to Christianity after David Livingstone emerged from the grotto alive and well, casting the tribes traditional beliefs and superstitions into doubt.

Thamaga ★★

About 12km (7 miles) beyond Kolobeng is a turn-off to the right to the village of Thamaga. In Thamaga just beyond the Botswelelo Centre is the **Thamaga Pottery shop** which sells handmade pottery kitchenware of the highest standard. Thamaga pottery has in fact created a very reputable name for itself with buyers from outside Botswana. This outlet is the hub of a localized pottery industry which includes the unusual works of **Pelegano Village Industries** in Gabane and the **Dinkgwana potters** located between Kanye and Lobatse.

Beyond Thamaga the road weaves its way through the hills, past the **Polokwe Viewing Point** towards the Trans-Kalahari Highway that heads for Namibia 700km (425 miles) away across the baking Kalahari sands. Upon reaching the highway, a right turn takes you 82km (51 miles) to **Jwaneng**, one of the richest diamond mines in the world, and another 519km (323 miles) beyond to **Ghanzi**. A left turn brings you to the large village of Kanye and a link through to Lobatse.

SOUTHWEST OF GABORONE
Kanye ★

This sprawling, picturesque village is the capital of the Bangwaketsi tribe. It was founded by **Chief Makaba** in the late 18th century as a well-defended hilltop settlement, (its name means 'to destroy' or 'to strike down'). The village was often under siege by various attackers, including **Mzilikazi** on his migration to Bulawayo and the German maverick **Jan Bloem**. But Kanye survived them all and is now an important and prosperous urban centre.

There are some good **traditional restaurants** in Kanye serving unique Batswana dishes. The **Ko Gae** ('My Home') café is situated on the side of the Kanye Hill and offers very genuine cuisine. The menu is in Setswana with English descriptions. A must are their popular **Seswaa** dishes – boiled and pounded beef – a local favourite often served at traditional celebrations such as weddings. The **Centre Hotel** has a more varied menu, though still with a distinctive Botswana flavour.

Lobatse ★

Lobatse, now home to some 70,000 people, was once considered to become Botswana's capital. It is a pleasant town nestling in a range of hills with a slightly wetter, cooler climate. Named after Chief Molebatse, Lobatse is home to the **Botswana Meat Commission**. Established in 1966 the Commission has a large abattoir, meat canning factory and leather tannery in Lobatse, as well as abattoirs in Francistown and Maun, from where they export quality 'Botswana Beef' to Europe, South Africa and various other countries throughout the world.

In the early 1960s Lobatse had the first tarmac road in Botswana; a few short kilometres laid especially for the Royal visit of the Duke and Duchess of Windsor. Located 70km (43 miles) from Gaborone, this charismatic 'cow' town is also the seat of the High Court of Botswana.

Otse and the Manyelanong Game Reserve ★★

The village of Otse is 15km (9 miles) outside Lobatse on the Gaborone road. North of the village is Otse Hill, the highest point in Botswana at 1489m (4885ft) above sea level. In the sheer cliffs beyond the settlement, the tiny Manyelanong Game Reserve protects a breeding colony of **Cape vultures**. The winter months are the best time to visit this reserve. There are now just under 60 breeding pairs of birds in the colony, but it is still one of the largest colonies of vultures in Botswana.

To get to the reserve, turn off the main Lobatse/Gaborone road in Otse at the Moeding College signpost. At the 'Y' junction turn right and keep heading for the high rocky hill.

> ### THE SOURCE OF THE LIMPOPO
>
> As described by Rudyard Kipling, the Limpopo River is a 'great gray-green greasy' expanse of coursing water surging across three countries towards the Indian Ocean. It is little known that the source of the Limpopo is just south of Gaborone near Lobatse, where it is called the Ngotwane River. As the Ngotwane River it forms the border between Botswana and South Africa, up to the Ngotwane Dam. This spills directly into the Gaborone Dam, from where the river continues its northeastern journey towards Parr's Halt. Here it changes its name to the Limpopo and again forms the national boundary up to the far eastern tip of the country where Botswana, Zimbabwe and South Africa meet at the confluence of the Limpopo and Shashe rivers.

Below: *Cape vultures* (Gyps coprotheres) *rest in a tree far from their cliff-edge roost.*

Gaborone and Surrounds at a Glance

Best Times to Visit

Gaborone can be oppressively **hot** in summer from **October** to **April** with temperatures often reaching 38ºC (100ºF). It can get especially hot between the intermittent **rainstorms**, which fall mainly between **December** and **February**. With Gaborone being relatively low lying (1000m/3281ft above sea level), the nights are also hot with an average drop in temperature of just 10ºC (18ºF). Winter can be cold, especially at night. Winter days are generally cool and cloudless.

Getting There

Air Botswana flies regularly between Johannesburg, Francistown, Maun and Kasane. Contact Air Botswana Central Reservations & ticket sales on tel: 395-1921, fax: 395-3928. **South African Express Airways** offers daily flights between Gaborone's Sir Seretse Khama International Airport and Johannesburg. Contact them at Game City on tel: 397-2397, fax: 397-2401. A host of international airlines fly into and out of Johannesburg and there are numerous Air Botswana and SA Express connections between 'Joburg' and Gaborone. In addition to air travel, Gaborone is just 360km (224 miles) from Johannesburg with very good road and rail links.

Getting Around

There are several **car-hire** companies in Gaborone: **Avis**,

tel: 397-5469, fax: 391-2205, e-mail: botswanares@avis.co.za **Budget**, tel: 390-2030, fax: 390-2028, e-mail: Botswana@budget.co.za **Imperial**, tel: 390-7233, fax: 390-4460. **Smart Car Rentals**, tel: 316-1116, fax: 316-1115.
Several **air charter** companies offer scheduled or special charter flights to tourist and business destinations. They include: **Kalahari Air Services**, tel: 395-1804, fax: 391-2015, e-mail: kasac@info.bw **NAC Botswana**, tel: 397-5257, fax: 397-5258, e-mail: les@info.bw, and **The Flying Mission**, tel: 390-0297, fax: 390-4181, e-mail: hanger@flyingmission.org.bw
Most hotels offer a bus **shuttle service** to and from the airport about 5km (3 miles) north of the city. Within the city the only form of public transport is private **mini-bus taxis**.
Botswana Railways runs a daily service to and from Lobatse and Pilane, and a day and overnight train to Francistown, with links to Bulawayo, Harare, Mafikeng and Johannesburg. The luxury **Blue Train** travels on occasion between Francistown and Gaborone as part of its southern African rail safari. For details contact Botswana Railways, tel: 395-1401.

Where to Stay

Gaborone
Luxury
Cresta President Hotel, Main

Mall, tel: 395-3631, fax: 395-1840, e-mail: respresident@cresta.co.bw Comfortable business hotel with conference facilities in the heart of the Main Mall.
Gaborone Sun, next to the Gaborone Golf Club, tel: 361-6000, fax: 390-2555, e-mail: gab_res@sunint.co.za Luxury rooms, fine restaurants and a buzzing casino.
Syringa Hotel, Mobuto Drive, tel: 319-0600, fax: 319-0660, e-mail: reservations@the syringahotel.co.bw Luxurious select services hotel with News Café near University.
Walmont Ambassador at the Grand Palm, tel: 363-7777, fax: 391-2989, e-mail: info@gp.walmont.com Outstanding luxury with excellent restaurants, casino and the Gaborone International Conference Centre (GICC). A member of Peermont Global Hotels and Resorts.
Mid-range
Cresta Lodge, Samora Machel Drive, tel: 397-5375, fax: 390-0635, e-mail: reslodge@cresta.co.bw Comfortable select services hotel in garden setting with the popular Chatters Restaurant.
Metcourt Inn at the Grand Palm, tel: 363-7777. Very comfortable limited services hotel, but with all access to the Grand Palm facilities.
Budget
Gaborone Hotel, tel: 392-2777, fax: 392-2727, e-mail: gabhot@info.bw Good value,

air conditioned and convenient central location next to shops, taxi rank and railway station.
Oasis Motel, Tlokweng Road, tel: 392-8396, fax: 392-8568, e-mail: oasismotel@botsnet.bw Choice of good value accommodation and famous Reflections restaurant.

Kanye
MID-RANGE
Motse Lodge & Cultural Village, tel: 548-0363, fax: 548-0370, e-mail: motselodge @botsnet.bw New cultural tourism establishment.

Lobatse
MID-RANGE
Cumberland Hotel, tel: 533-0281, fax: 533-2106, e-mail: Cumberland@botsnet.bw Comfortable hotel with pool and good à la carte restaurant.

Phakalane
LUXURY
Phakalane Golf Hotel Resort, in Phakalane Golf Estate, tel: 393-0000, fax: 393-8918, e-mail: sales@phakalane.co.bw Luxury accommodation and the ultimate golfing experience.

WHERE TO EAT

There are many restaurants and takeaways in Gaborone – the following is just a small selection. As Botswana is a prime beef producer, the steaks are usually excellent, and most hotels serve good roast carveries as well as

traditional *seswaa* and *pap*.
The Boulevard, Phakalane, tel: 393-3803. Pub and restaurant.
Bull and Bush, tel: 397-5070. Famous steakhouse and pub in relaxed garden setting.
Caravela Portuguese Restaurant, tel: 391-4284. Excellent Portuguese food with indoor and outdoor seating.
Dros, tel: 371-0091. Franchised restaurant and wine bar in Molapo Crossing Mall.
Delis, in the Craft Workshop, tel: 395-7933. Italian deli and coffee shop; excellent lunches.
Drotsky's, Phakalane Golf Club, tel: 393-0000. Fine cuisine and outstanding wines.
Falcon Restaurant, in the Falcon Crest Lodge, tel: 393-5373. Open 7 days a week.
Maharaja, tel: 391-1060. Authentic Indian cuisine.
News Café, Syringa Hotel, tel: 319-0666. Quality international franchise restaurant and popular nightspot.
The Noodle House, Mowana Park shopping centre, Phakalane, tel: 390-0845. Chinese with takeaway.
Primi-Piatti, River Walk Mall, tel: 370-0068. Great Italian themed restaurant.
Sanitas Garden Centre, tel:

395-2538. Wholesome lunches and teas served in the garden with wonderful playground for the children.

TOURS AND EXCURSIONS

Arne's Horse Safaris, tel: 390-9091. Trails through the hills north of Gaborone.
Mokolodi Nature Reserve, tel: 316-1955, fax: 316-5488. Rhino tracking, elephant walks, game drives, bush braais, more.
Gaborone Game Reserve, good bird and game viewing.

USEFUL CONTACTS

All-in-Hiring, tel: 395-2686, tents and camping equipment.
Outdoor World, tel: 397-4780. Stockists of camping supplies.
Botswana Society, tel: 391-9673. Botswana history and conservation.
Parks & Reserves Reservations, tel: 318-0774.
Department of Tourism, tel: 395-3024.
Kalahari Conservation Society, tel: 397-4557.
Gaborone Private Hospital, tel: 390-1999.
MRI Medical Rescue, tel: 390-1601, e-mail: medrescue @info.bw Essential short-term medical care and evacuation.

GABORONE	J	F	M	A	M	J	J	A	S	O	N	D
MIN AVE TEMP. °C	20	19	17	13	8	5	4	7	12	16	18	19
MIN AVE TEMP. °F	68	66	63	55	46	41	39	45	54	61	65	66
MAX AVE TEMP. °C	33	32	30	27	25	22	23	26	29	31	32	32
MAX AVE TEMP. °F	91	90	86	81	77	72	73	79	84	88	90	90
RAINFALL mm	104	86	58	50	11	4	4	4	17	46	75	73
RAINFALL in	4.1	3.4	2.3	2	0.4	0.2	0.2	0.2	0.7	1.8	3	2.9

3
The Southern Kalahari

The Kalahari is a vast semidesert which, unlike true deserts, does receive erratic rainfall. It remains, however, a harsh and inhospitable place. There is sufficient vegetation and grass cover to sustain considerable wildlife populations, but the lack of water has forced nature to adapt, and in this fascinating and remote corner of the country visitors find a unique ecology perfectly adapted to the challenging climate. Mankind is, however, less adaptable and, apart from the nomadic San, the region has remained untouched, protected from the encroaching cattleposts, which fortunately remain water dependent.

THE KGALAGADI TRANSFRONTIER PARK ★★★

The Gemsbok National Park was the first national park to be established in Botswana back in 1937 to protect the fragile environment and the large herds of wildlife that roamed the area. In 2000 this park was amalgamated with the Kalahari Gemsbok National Park on the South African side to form Africa's first formally declared transborder conservation area – the Kgalagadi Transfrontier Park (KTP). This new park with a combined area of about 38,000km² (14,670 sq miles), three quarters of which is in Botswana, was launched by South African President Thabo Mbeki and Botswana President Festus Mogae.

The Mabuasehube Area

In 1995 Mabuasehube Game Reserve, with its network of roads and camping facilities was amalgamated into the Gemsbok National Park. This Mabuasehube area

DON'T MISS

★★★ **Western Woodlands:** camp in an idyllic natural woodland in a remote uninhabited region.
★★★ Finding **cheetah** at the kill.
★★ Watching **leopard** stalking across the open pans.
★★ **Nossob River Valley:** exciting drives.
★ The rare **brown hyena**.
★ **Bat-eared foxes** coming out to play in the evening.
★ The herds of **gemsbok**.

Opposite: *The massive rapier-horned gemsbok* (Oryx gazella) *is perfectly adapted to the harsh Kalahari environment.*

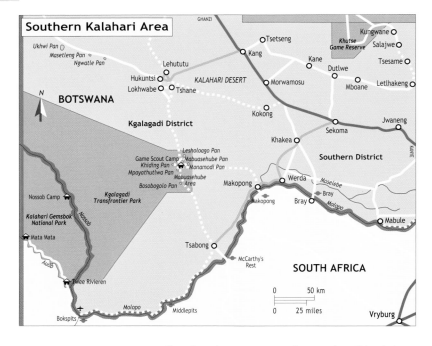

Southern Kalahari Area

GHANZI

Kungwane ○

○Tsetseng   *Khutse*   Salajwe ○
                   Game Reserve

Ukhwi Pan ○   ○ Kang   Kane   Tsesame ○
Masetleng Pan ○   ○
  Ngwatle Pan ○   Lehututu   Dutlwe
                                                                 ○   Letlhakeng ○
            Hukuntsi ○   *KALAHARI DESERT*   ○Morwamosu   Mboane
            Lokhwabe ○ ○Tshane

N   **BOTSWANA**
                                                        ○
                                                      Kokong   Jwaneng
            Kgalagadi District   ○
                                                                 ○
                                                              Sekoma

                                               Khakea ○   KANYE

                              Lesholoago Pan
            Game Scout Camp Mabuasehube Pan   **Southern District**
              Khiding Pan   ○ Monamodi Pan
          Mpayathutlwa Pan   Mabuasehube
                Bosobogolo Pan ○ Area   Makopong   ○ Werda   *Moselebe*
Nossob Camp   ○   ○ Bray
            Kgalagadi   Makopong   Bray ○   *Molopo*
            Transfrontier Park

Kalahari Gemsbok   ○ Mabule
National Park   *Nossob*

Mata Mata

            Auob   Tsabong ○

                                          ● McCarthy's
                                             Rest   **SOUTH AFRICA**

                                                      0   50 km
                                                      |———————|
                                                      0   25 miles

            Molopo   Middlepits   Vryburg ○
Bokspits

---

offers the adventurous traveller a truly wild safari experience and is currently the only accessible portion of the Transfrontier Park, although there are plans for new tracks and camel trails into the uncharted wilderness towards the Nossob in the heart of the Park.

The Pans ★★★

The Transfrontier Park's Mabuasehube area is dotted with numerous **pans** the major ones of which are easily accessible off the main road. Some of these pans offer camping facilities and picnic sites.

Approaching the park from Tsabong in the south, the first pan reached is **Bosobogolo**. The **Game Scout Camp** is in the middle of the Mabuasehube area near **Mpayathutlwa Pan**. This is the only place where **water** is available. All visitors must register at the Game Scout Camp as soon as they arrive in the area.

There is a scenic camping and picnic site on a high dune overlooking Mpayathutlwa Pan. This elevated and shady vantage point gives an excellent view across the pan on which a water hole is located. **Monamodi Pan**, which is part of an ancient fossil valley complex, is to the east and is accessible by a signposted track.

Mabuasehube Pan is about 7km (4 miles) north of the Scout Camp. There are two camp sites overlooking the pan, both with barbecue sites and long-drop toilets. Mabuasehube Pan also has a water hole which pumps water into a small reservoir for the game. As one approaches Mabuasehube Pan from the main road there is a steep descent with a rocky cliff face to the left. This is a favourite leopard haunt.

Khiding Pan and its camp site are further to the west and the sandy track to this pan passes through typical grassy thornscrub.

The most northerly pan is **Lesholoago** which is 8km (5 miles) to the east of the main road.

Park Rules

The Game Scout Camp at Mpayathutlwa is open during the following times: March–September, 06:30–18:30; October–February, 05:30 to 19:30.
● No driving is allowed within the park outside these hours, and within these hours the speed limit is 40kph (24mph).
● Off-road driving is strictly prohibited as is driving on the pan surface.
● Do not feed the animals as they will inevitably have to be destroyed.
● Stay in your vehicle except at designated camping or picnic sites.
● Firearms and spotlights are not permitted.

Routes to the Kgalagadi Transfrontier Park

The most commonly used route into the Mabuasehube area of the Transfrontier Park is via Tsabong. From Gaborone drive to Jwaneng, via either Lobatse and Kanye, or through Mogoditshane and Thamaga. Jwaneng is the last place with reliable supplies and provisions.

From Jwaneng continue west through Sekoma to Khakea. Khakea is a short distance off the main road, signposted to the left, but you can't miss it as the village nestles under a tall telecommunications tower. There is a store here selling basic commodities and usually petrol. From Khakea the road takes you south through the villages of Werda and Makopong, onto Tsabong. The whole journey from Gaborone is 478km (287 miles).

Below: *Ostriches are ideally suited to the dry Kalahari conditions and there are numerous ostrich farms in the Ghanzi and Kgalagadi Districts.*

Above: *Campers enjoy the cool Kalahari desert air as the day draws to a close.*
Opposite bottom: *The pods of the camel thorn tree* (Acacia erioloba). *The name is a corruption of the Afrikaans, meaning 'giraffe thorn'.*

From Tsabong take the northern track to Tshane. The road is extremely sandy and four-wheel-drive is essential. The Transfrontier Park boundary sign is 76km (47 miles) from Tsabong, and the Scout Camp a further 45km (28 miles) into the park. This short stretch from Tsabong will take at least four hours to negotiate.

The northern route into the reserve is via Tshane, reached from Maun via Ghanzi or from Gaborone via Kang. The 278km (170-mile) road from Ghanzi to Kang is good tar, as is the 104km (62-mile) road from Kang to Tshane, but thereafter the track from Tshane to Tsabong is extremely sandy. To find the route drive through Tshane down to Tshane Pan where you take the track which turns due south.

THE SOUTH AFRICAN SIDE OF THE PARK ★★
This portion of the twin-park lies in South Africa and covers over 8300km² (3204 sq miles) of harsh sandveld.

Rest Camps
There are three established rest camps on the South African side of the park. The main camp at **Twee Rivieren** has excellent amenities and a tarred airstrip.

Along the Auob River at the Namibian border is the **Mata Mata rest camp**. The amenities here are limited with only camping facilities being offered, but these are comfortable and petrol is available. Along the Nossob River north of the entrance gate is the **Nossob rest camp**. Nossob also has an airstrip for fly-in visitors.

Details of park entrance times can be confirmed through the South African National Parks Board on tel: (+27 12) 428-9111, fax: (+27 12) 426-5500, e-mail: reservations@sanparks.org or by writing to P.O. Box 787, Pretoria 0001, South Africa. All reservations must be made through this office.

WHEEL WARY

When driving in the park you must be sure to reduce the tyre pressure of your vehicle. This will give you better traction in the sand and reduces the corrugating effect on the roads. As you will need to reinflate your tyres upon reaching the tar road on your way out, it is advisable to carry at least a portable foot pump.

GHANZI

Ghanzi, known as the 'Capital of the Kalahari', is more the capital of cattle country, as with its fine grazing and abundant groundwater it is reputed to be the best beef range in the world. Although it has never been a tourist destination, in Ghanzi you will find **Ghanzi Craft** which is an outlet and training centre for San craftspeople who sell outstanding works at a fraction of the city prices.

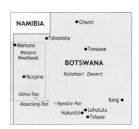

Situated 37km (23 miles) from Ghanzi on the Maun road is the tiny village of **D'Kar** where you will also find the Kuru Museum and Cultural Centre which is definitely worth visiting.

THE WESTERN WOODLANDS ★★

This vast almost totally uninhabited area along the southwestern edge of Botswana is one of the least known in southern Africa. Here, a remarkable cluster of mature **camel thorn trees** (*Acacia erioloba*) is set in golden grasslands spreading over an area of about 160km² (60 sq miles) in a strip almost 40km (24 miles) long. With virtually no undergrowth the impression given is that of a vast carefully tended park offering numerous idyllic camp sites.

As this area is not in a national park, booking and registration are not required. However, it is one of the planet's last pristine wildernesses, so take care of it.

Routes to the Woodlands

There are few roads and those to be found in this expanse are little more than undefined tracks. There are hardly any supply points, except for fuel and basic commodities at Hukuntsi, Mamuno at the Namibian border post, and Kang on the Trans-Kalahari Highway, so all visitors must be self-sufficient with reserves of water and fuel, as well as a compass and basic spares in case of a breakdown.

THE JEWELS OF JWANENG

Jwaneng is a new town northwest of Gaborone. Before 1980 the area consisted of only a few cattleposts, but is now home to over 15,000 people. The town was built in the early 1980s to house employees of Jwaneng mine after diamonds were discovered there in 1976. There is a large multicored kimberlitic pipe at Jwaneng, making this young but rapidly growing mine one of the richest in the world. The open-cast mine pit at Jwaneng is much larger than the famous 'Big Hole' in Kimberley.

THE CUTLINE GRID

In the 1970s and '80s De Beers did a lot of diamond prospecting in the south and western areas of Botswana including the Kgalagadi Transfrontier Park. With graders they cut a chequered grid of north– south and east–west tracks across the country, each at roughly 15km (9-mile) intervals. Many of these lines are now overgrown, but others are kept open as roads. If while driving through the Kgalagadi Transfrontier Park you notice that the road is perfectly straight, you are probably driving on one of these old prospecting cutlines.

Right: *After the short rains, Devil's thorn flowers paint the road from Tshane to Mabuasehube.*

The best route from Gaborone is via Kang, 240km (144 miles) northwest of Jwaneng on the Ghanzi road. At Kang turn west to Tshane. This is a tarred road of 115km (70 miles) from Kang to Hukuntsi, which is the last spot of civilization as you head west. The road from Hukuntsi to Ncojane is being upgraded from the undefined track it used to be, but check the state of the road with the Department of Roads in Gaborone on tel: 391-3511 (enquiries) or 395-6230 (rural roads) before departing, and do not attempt the journey without four wheel drive.

Within the first 40km (24 miles) there are five large pans all with sand dunes overlooking their southern edges. After a further 33km (20 miles) of flat sandveld, **Ngwaatle Pan** is reached. There is a small San village here, one of the only human settlements in the region. 28km (17 miles) beyond Ngwaatle and 90km (54 miles) from Hukuntsi lies **Masetleng Pan** which in the early 1990s was the site of concerted oil exploration.

The Western Woodlands are 10km (6 miles) northwest of the pan. There is no road to the woodlands and you will have to try the various tracks, but the whole area around Matsetleng can be explored and there are other equally inspiring spots waiting to be discovered. The road northwest goes on to the San village of Ukwi which is near Ukwi Pan which is reputed to be one of the largest pans in Botswana outside of the Makgadikgadi. It weaves on through to the Ncojane Farms and eventually on to the Namibian border post at Mamuno.

Southern Kalahari at a Glance

Summers from **September** to **April** are scorching **hot** with very little rain. The evenings are a bit cooler, but can still be uncomfortably warm. In addition, there is a plethora of pollen and grass seeds in the air, so it is not a good time for anyone susceptible to hayfever. During winter the days are very hot often reaching the 30ºC (86ºF) mark, but nights can be bitterly cold with heavy frosts and the rare light snowfall. Because of the seasonal migratory patterns of the game, **game viewing** is better in different places during the various times of the year. The best times for game viewing in the South African and western Botswana areas is from March to May. In the eastern and Mabuasehube areas the best time to see game is from September to May. But it is extremely hot so try to avoid January to March.

GETTING THERE

There are airstrips at Ghanzi, Tsabong, Twee Rivieren and Nossob Camp. The best route to the Mabuasehube part of the Transfrontier Park is north from Tsabong. Or to get to the South African side of the park cross the border at Ramatlabama and drive to Twee Rivieren via Kuruman.

GETTING AROUND

The park and wilderness areas on the Botswana side are only accessible with 4x4s. On the South African side the main routes are surfaced and can be traversed with ordinary cars. Hire vehicles at Twee Rivieren.

WHERE TO STAY

There are camp sites with barbecues and long-drop toilets at the pans in the Mabuasehube area. On the South African side the SA Parks Board maintains luxury chalets at Twee Rivieren and serviced camp sites with basic facilities at Nossob and Mata Mata camps.

CAMPING

Camping at the pans outside the national park is permitted, but if it is in a populated area be sure to ask permission from the local chief or headman. Camp sites are available at the **Kalahari Arms Hotel** and at the **Kang Ultra Stop**.

Ghanzi

Kalahari Arms Hotel, tel: 659-6298. Comfortable rondavels with *en-suite* facilities, restaurant, pool and bar.
Tautona Lodge, tel: 659-7499, fax: 659-7500, e-mail: tautonalodge@botsnet.bw New thatched lodge.

Jwaneng

Mokala Lodge, tel: 588-0835. Comfortable accommodation and good food.

Kang

Kang Ultra-Stop, tel: 651-7292/6/7. Range of accommodation with swimming pool, good restaurant and bar. Booking is essential.

Tsabong

Desert Motel, tel: 654-0020, e-mail: motel@mega.bw Double and single rooms available 2km (1.2 miles) north of Tsabong.

WHERE TO EAT

There is a good restaurant and takeaway at Twee Rivieren, otherwise there are no other facilities in the KTP or woodlands area (not even water), so visitors must be totally self sufficient. The best restaurant in the area is at Kang on the Trans-Kalahari Highway.

TOURS AND EXCURSIONS

Most reputable safari operators can tailor specific trips into the area, but there are no regular tours.

TSABONG	J	F	M	A	M	J	J	A	S	O	N	D
MIN AVE TEMP. ºC	19	19	17	12	6	4	4	5	9	13	16	18
MIN AVE TEMP. ºF	66	66	63	54	43	39	39	41	48	55	61	64
MAX AVE TEMP. ºC	35	34	32	28	25	22	22	25	29	31	33	35
MAX AVE TEMP. ºF	95	93	90	82	77	72	72	77	84	88	91	95
RAINFALL mm	53	59	51	37	12	4	1	3	5	21	33	33
RAINFALL in	2.1	2.3	2	1.5	0.5	0.2	0	0.1	0.2	0.8	1.3	1.3

4
The Makgadikgadi Pans

In this modern world of cities and overpopulation, it is almost impossible to imagine a place of wide open, uninhabited spaces under an endless canopy of blue sky.

The Makgadikgadi is such a place. The largest salt pan in the world, its silver-grey surface covers over 12,000km² (7500 sq miles) of completely barren flatness, an area almost the size of Portugal.

This vast complex bears testimony to the superlake that once covered much of northern Botswana. Thousands of years ago the courses of the Chobe and Zambezi rivers were diverted from the lake and, as it shrank, so the water's salinity increased. All that was left was the sun-baked bed. Today, it is at the Makgadikgadi that visitors find the true peace and serenity of complete isolation.

It is possible that there are still remote areas left to be discovered, while other areas have been occupied for thousands of years, rich with the remains of prehistoric settlements. Vast migrating herds of animals traverse the area and in the wet season thousands of water birds flock to the pans.

There are numerous pans in the Makgadikgadi, but the three major pans are: **Ntwetwe Pan** south of Gweta, the largest pan in the system; **Sowa Pan** southwest of Nata; and **Nxai Pan** north of the main Gweta/Maun road.

There are few serviced facilities in the Makgadikgadi and, although there are landing strips at both Gweta and Nata, it is an area more suited to self-sufficient 4WD parties. To reach these remote areas most people will pass through Francistown, the gateway to northern Botswana.

DON'T MISS

★★★ Being surrounded by **flamingoes** in a sea of pink.
★★★ **Sowa Pan:** a 4WD cruise under a full moon.
★★★ **Kubu Island:** witness a golden sunrise.
★★ Watching massive herds of **migrating zebra**.
★★ **Baines' Baobabs:** spectacular after rainfall.
★★ Speeding across the pans on a quad-bike.
★ Discovering the signatures of old explorers on ancient **baobab trees**.

Opposite: *The shallow water of the rain-filled Makgadikgadi reflects an expansive sky.*

FRANCISTOWN

As one of the oldest towns in Botswana and site of southern Africa's first gold rush, Francistown, home to 100,000 people, is a typical frontier town. It manages to maintain its character despite being Botswana's second-largest urban centre and '**Capital of the North**'.

Evidence of human habitation goes back for 80,000 years, but it was only in the 1860s when the geologist **Karl Mauch** discovered **gold** at Tati that the town was established. Soon after the initial discoveries at Tati, more gold deposits were discovered at Francistown. Prospectors rushed into the area from as far away as Australia expecting Francistown to be the Ophir of Africa.

The town was named after **Daniel Francis** who came to Tati in the 1860s and organized the establishment of the town through the sale of freehold stands to the public.

Initially the town consisted of just one main street running parallel to the 'Cape to Cairo' railway along which there were numerous bustling stores and rowdy saloons. Many reminders of this bygone era are preserved in the evocative mine names which remain, such as 'Bonanza', 'Jim's Luck', 'Lady Mary', 'Phoenix', and 'White Elephant'.

CLIMATE

The Makgadikgadi is very hot in the summer months from October to May, relieved by infrequent showers and thunderstorms. If there is water in the pans they can become uncomfortably humid with the high level of evaporation. In winter, from June to September, the days are warm but the nights can be bitterly cold with temperatures dropping to well below freezing. In October the area is prone to windstorms and can be very dusty.

Left: *The busy, shop-lined Blue Jacket street which runs through the middle of Francistown.*

BLUE JACKET

'Blue Jacket' is the name of not only a mine, but also the main street running through Francistown. It is in memory of an old prospector, Sam Andersen, who had become famous (before arriving in Botswana) as the first man to cross the western desert in Australia on foot with his prospecting wheelbarrow. The name 'Blue Jacket' came into existence because of Sam's habit of always wearing a blue denim jacket wherever he went.

The gold in eastern Botswana is a complex mix of narrow reefs, difficult for early miners to extract; by the 1940s much of the small-scale mining had ceased. Today, there is little in the way of gold mining in Francistown, although a mine recently established west of the city has brought new life to the local industry.

Located at the head of the railway line and the junction of the Maun/Kasane and Bulawayo roads, Francistown has been a natural growth point and now boasts considerable commercial and industrial enterprises, including the **Botswana Meat Commission** abattoir which processes a great deal of Botswana's beef for export to Europe and South Africa. There are a couple of good hotels, a casino, sophisticated shopping malls, night clubs, one of the largest referral hospitals in Botswana, a library, well-kept parks, and colourful markets, which, combined with the town's friendly reputation, makes it a pleasant and comfortable stopover.

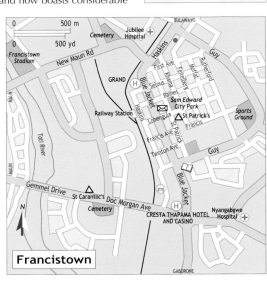

Opposite: *The pic-
turesque village of Nata
near the edge of the
Makgadikgadi.*
Below: *A flotilla of pelicans
fishing in the shallows of
the Nata Bird Sanctuary.*

Museum Supa-Ngwao ★★

The Museum Supa-Ngwao is the cultural centre of northeastern Botswana with exhibits depicting the heritage of
the local people and the history of Francistown itself.
There is also a tourist information centre and a craft shop
at the museum, located near the central ring road. Open
08:00–13:00 and 14:00–17:00 Monday–Friday, 09:00–
17:00 Saturday; tel: 240-3088, e-mail: snm@info.bw

NORTH OF FRANCISTOWN

The village of Nata lies 187km (113 miles) from
Francistown, but some 15km (9 miles) before this traditional village is the entrance to the Nata Sanctuary.

Nata Bird Sanctuary ★★★

This 230km^2 (90 sq mile) sanctuary was established in the
early 1990s on the far northeastern edge of Sowa Pan
and, apart from the Makgadikgadi and Nxai Pan National
Park, is the only protected reserve in the area. It is a local
community project managed by a board of trustees
selected from four nearby villages. This unique approach
to community involvement in ecotourism is considered to
be the key to conservation throughout Africa.

A **camp site** with barbecue sites, hot showers and flush
toilets can be found near the park entrance. There are
numerous camp sites, each carefully positioned for both
shade and the panoramic view across the pre-pan grasslands, where the many birds that the sanctuary has
become famous for can be seen. The
sanctuary is open daily from 07:00–19:00

During the wet season the Nata River
carries water from Zimbabwe into Sowa
Pan, filling its northern region and attracting a variety of **water birds**. This area is
also an important breeding ground for
flamingoes and **pelicans**. In the dry winter
months bustards and korhaans can be
seen in the grass fringes of the pan
accompanied by migratory birds such as
kites, eagles and bee-eaters.

While the roads throughout the sanctuary are well maintained, access to certain areas may be restricted to four-wheel-drive, particularly in the wet season when the black cotton soil can become treacherous.

Nata Village ★★
This traditional village, set on the Nata River banks, is very scenic with decorated huts and administrative buildings in a grove of Ilala palms.

Sowa Pan Lodge ★
Sowa Pan Lodge is located on the northern edge of Nata village at the Maun turn-off, and offers chalets and camping facilities with a restaurant and takeaway.

Nata Lodge ★★
Nata Lodge is set in a grove of Ilala palms 10km (6 miles) outside Nata on the Francistown road. It is a popular lodge, famous for its 'sunset cruises' onto Sowa Pan.

At the lodge are several A-frame chalets, tented accommodation and good camping facilities. There is a curio shop, an excellent restaurant, a swimming pool with a bar, and a patio where meals are served under the shade of huge morula and monkey-thorn trees. These monkey-thorn trees are home to numerous squirrels as well as a family of nocturnal bushbabies sometimes seen in the evenings taking offerings from the bar.

THE PINK TIDE

Every year after the rains, when the eastern edge of Sowa Pan fills with water the 'Pink Tide' comes in. Thousands of greater and lesser **flamingoes** *(Phoenicopterus ruber and Phoenicopterus minor)* flock to the pans which are the largest breeding site for greater flamingoes in Africa. The greater flamingoes feed on brine shrimps, worms and crustaceans and nest on islands, while the lesser flamingoes feed on algae and build tall, mud-cone nests on the pan surface, just as the water is receding. These cones protect the chicks from the severe heat. The heat is, however, not the only hazard they face; before the young birds are able to fly the water dries up, forcing their parents to walk them sometimes as far as 150km (90 miles) to the last of the water in northern Sowa. Many of the babies die on the way, but this strange cycle is endlessly repeated.

SOWA'S SODA ASH

Just beneath the surface of Sowa Pan are vast quantities of **soda ash**, used in the manufacture of glass, ceramics, soap and paper as well as being a useful cleaning agent. With the obvious economic potential of this natural resource, in the early 1990s a new town was built on the **Sowa Spit** to service a massive mining operation on the pan. The plant included the construction of 55 wells in a wellfield covering 200km² (125 sq miles). The project was, however, placed in provisional liquidation in 1995. New investors relaunched the operation under the name **Botash**. This preserved many jobs, but with dropping international prices and unfavourable exchange rates Botash is unlikely to be the economic booster it was hoped to be.

SOWA PAN ★★★

Sowa (or Sua) is the bushman word for salt, an apt description of this vast white expanse.

Most visitors only access the eastern edge of Sowa Pan with short forays onto the outstretched surface from Nata Lodge or the Bird Sanctuary, but it is a vast area with several days being required to fully appreciate it.

There are very few rock islands in the Makgadikgadi, but in southern Sowa a scattering of granite isles lie on the white surface like beached whales. All have unique characteristics that give this desolate place its mesmeric attraction. Of all the islands, Kubu is the most famous.

Kubu Island ★★★

Rising no more than 20m (70ft) above the pan, this national monument with its fossil beaches, stunted baobab trees and mysterious stone walls, leaves an indelible impression upon all who visit its water-worn shores. Many of Kubu's rocks are stained white with fossilized bird droppings. This ancient guano is called apatite and bears testimony to a large bird population that used to live on the island, feeding off the fish of the waters that surrounded their rocky knoll.

There is a trig-beacon on the island's summit. The rocks on the northeastern side are all smoothed by wave action, while on the opposite leeward side are thousands of small, rounded pebbles, which used to protrude as a tiny wave-washed beach. As the level of this immense inland sea rose and fell, there were times when Kubu was deep beneath the waves, others when it lay exposed in a sea of sand and others when it hardly showed above the surface, surrounded by 100km (60 miles) of sea.

There are no camping facilities on Kubu or the other islands of southwestern Sowa, but there are many idyllic spots overlooking the pan. Campers must bring their own firewood and must remove all their litter. A further 38km (24 miles) to the east lies the seldom-visited **Kukonje Island**.

Below: *In years of good rain Sowa Pan attracts hundreds of thousands of greater and lesser flamingoes.*

Routes to Kubu Island

There are several routes to Kubu, all requiring four-wheel-drive, but most travel agents or tour operators can organize special trips to Kubu for those without.

The easiest route to Kubu is from Francistown. Take the Orapa road from Francistown and continue for 200km (125 miles) until you reach a dirt road which intersects with the

Above: *The stunted, salt-stained baobabs of Kubu guard the island's rocky beaches.*

main road. There is a sign indicating Letlhakane to the left. At the crossroads take the road to the right, to the village of Mmatshumo.

Drive through the village keeping to the main northern track. This is the track to the pans, Thabatshukudu village and eventually the Nata/Maun road. A short distance beyond Mmatshumo the road descends the escarpment giving a breaktaking view of the pan. Approximately 26km (16 miles) out of Mmatshumo is an unmarked track to the right. Take this turn-off and Kubu is 18km (11 miles) further on. For those with GPS the co-ordinates are 20°53'50" S latitude and 25°49'41" E longitude.

The ruined stone wall on Kubu encloses what appears to have been an uninhabited area. Archaeologists consider it to have been a ritualistic initiation site.

There is much greater evidence of ancient human habitation near the village of Mosu, south of Kubu Island.

Mosu *

This scenic palm-lined village overlooks the sprawling pan from the edge of a 40m (130ft) escarpment. It is here that one of Botswana's greatest **archaeological sites** has been discovered.

It is an extremely remote and inaccessible place but, for the historically inclined, it is an amazing area where new discoveries can be made around almost every corner. Virtually every headland overlooking the pan, or sea as it was, on the shores of southern Sowa is the site of an ancient settlement.

ARCHAEOLOGIST'S PARADISE

There has been little archaeological research in northern Botswana but there are countless sites of interest around the Makgadikgadi, including ancient settlements and rich fossil beds.On the pans you will find Stone Age tools, while fossilized papyrus stems and mollusc shells litter the surrounding areas. In the west near the Boteti River are areas which are scattered with Stone Age tools and hand axes. With the premium for suitable stone, local residents in these regions collect the stones in piles, selling them off for building material. Possibly as many as 10% of the rocks in these piles are actually hand-chipped Stone Age tools, which are being sold off as cheap building materials.

Above: *A herd of springbok shares a water hole on Nxai Pan with a flock of birds.*
Opposite: *As there are hardly any landmarks in the Makgadikgadi, visitors crossing the pans must be totally self-sufficient.*

GETTING UNSTUCK

Getting stuck in a pan is a common problem and it can take hours or sometimes days to dig your way out. Even if you have a winch there is nothing to attach it to on the flat featureless pan surface. In this situation, dig a hole to the exact size of your spare wheel 6m (20ft) away and at right angles to the front of your vehicle. Attach the winch to the spare wheel and sink it into the hole. This should provide a suitable anchor for the winch to extract your vehicle.

Gweta ★★

The quaint village of Gweta is an established settlement near **Ntwetwe Pan**, 100km (60 miles) from Nata on the main Maun road. It is a dry, dusty spot, but its name, which means 'place of the big frogs', implies a wetter past. In years of exceptional rain, bullfrogs are still reputed to miraculously appear in the village. There is a petrol station, a general dealer and a liquor store in Gweta.

Gweta Rest Camp ★★

This collection of chalets is gathered around an inviting swimming pool, bar, curio shop and thatched restaurant. It is from here that one can explore the Makgadikgadi in a variety of unusual ways; the lodge offers guided horse trails, vehicle excursions and quad-bike trips, as well as overnight safaris onto the pans or further afield.

Jack's Camp ★★★

Between Gweta and the Makgadikgadi and Nxai Pan National Park, on the edge of Ntwetwe Pan and nestling in a palm oasis, lies Jack's Camp. Winner of the UK's prestigious Sunday Times Travel Magazine Award for 'Best Resort – Outstanding Service', Jack's has a distinctive 1940s flavour, evoking the original safari experience combined with modern luxury.

THE MAKGADIKGADI AND NXAI PAN NATIONAL PARK ★★★

In 1993 the area of the Nxai Pan National Park was extended south to the main Gweta/Maun road, amalgamating it with the Makgadikgadi Pans Game Reserve. It was renamed 'The Makgadikgadi and Nxai Pan National Park' to form one vast unfenced park covering just under 7500km^2 (2850 sq miles).

Four-wheel-drive is recommended throughout this area, as even in the dry season the pan surface can be treacherous with the unseen water table lurking often just inches under the hard-baked surface. Once on the pans the exhilaration of speeding across the flat surface is unforgettable.

While there are no fixed lodges or hotels in the park, there are several designated camp sites. This limits access to all but the fully equipped self-drive visitor, or those on tailor-made safaris.

Xhumaga Camp Site ★

In the southern section of the park there are two camp sites. One is at Xhumaga overlooking the Boteti River and Hippo Pool No. 1 near the Game Scout Camp on the extreme western edge of the park. At this camp site is an observation platform overlooking the river and a grove of acacia trees providing good shade even in the height of summer. There is an ablution block with running bore-hole water and cold showers. Visitors should bring their own firewood or use gas cookers.

Njuca Camp Site ★

The second camp site is near the east of the park, 40km (24 miles) from Xhumaga and 20km (12 miles) from the Game Scout Camp on the low Njuca hills. In most places these 'hills' would be little more than unnamed undulations, but on the perfectly level Makgadikgadi their slight elevation affords incredible views of up to 15km (9 miles) across the shimmering pan. There are pit latrines at Njuca, but **no water**.

THE BAOBAB TRAIL

With the almost total absence of landmarks in the Makgadikgadi, the huge baobab trees which grow there became points of

BUSHMAN PITS

Near the village of Phuduhudu there are numerous hand-dug holes and wells. These were dug by the San not only for water but also as hides from which they could ambush passing game with poison-tipped arrows. Take the old gravel Nata/Maun road west from Phuduhudu for about 10km (6 miles) and you'll find the sprawled ruins of an old cattlepost under a collection of huge shady trees. The pits are in the immediate vicinity. Zebra and wildebeest often rest under the trees on their way to and from the pans.

THE UPSIDE-DOWN TREE

The baobab *(Adansonia digitata)* tree can grow to over 40m (130ft) in diameter. There are countless legends about the baobab; the Bushmen believe that there are no young baobabs, but that God throws fully grown ones down from heaven. Unfortunately being top-heavy they always land with their roots in the air. Another is that the hyena is responsible for its appearance. When God planted trees on earth he gave one to each animal. The hyena was last in line and was left with the strange-looking baobab. In disgust he pulled it out of the ground and replanted it upside down! Reputed to grow up to 4000 years old, these giants have numerous nutritional and medicinal properties. Their leaves are rich in vitamin C and they store incredible volumes of water both in their wood and in hollows in their trunks.

navigation for early explorers and, around the pans, almost every great baobab can tell a fascinating story through the old signatures carved into it. Take the time to stop and study any of the larger specimens and you're bound to be rewarded.

On the northern edge of Ntwetwe near Gutsha Pan is **Green's Baobab**, which bears not only the signatures of 'Green's Expedition' dated 1858–1859, but also an elusive 'H.V.Z. – 1851/2', which some consider could have been carved by the flamboyant Hendrick Van Zyl, founder of the town of Ghanzi.

Some 7km (4 miles) from Green's Baobab is another monster visible from up to 20km (12 miles) away, which entices the imagination with a gothic 'J.C.'. However, these are the initials of James Chapman who passed this way with the painter Thomas Baines in 1862.

In the middle of the spreading trunk of this great tree is a hollow recess which was used as a post box by many early travellers, a habit which led to this meeting place becoming known as the Post Office Tree. More famous than these trees, however, are Baines' Baobabs.

Both Baines' Baobabs and Kudiakam Pan, over which they look, are in the northern section of the Makgadikgadi Pans Game Reserve. There is only one track into this part of the reserve which turns off the Nata/Maun road 77km (46 miles) from Gweta and 135km (81 miles) before Maun.

The sandy track is only navigable by four-wheel-drive. After 15km (9 miles) there is a cross road, which is the

original Nata/Maun road. A left turn takes you to the village of **Phuduhudu**, while right takes you to Baines' Baobabs. Continue straight to reach the Game Scout Camp which is a further 18km (11 miles) along this track. All visitors must report either here or to the Makgadikgadi gate to pay entrance and camping fees before visiting any area within the park, including Baines' Baobabs. Just beyond the entrance gate the road winds up a series of sand dunes. The dunes' summit rises about 20m (65ft) above the plain and it is from here that one is greeted by the first view across the expanse of Nxai Pan.

Baines' Baobabs ★★★

This remarkable cluster of trees, also known as the Seven Sisters, has been immortalized by photographers and painters over the years, including Prince Charles, but they were made famous by the painter and naturalist Thomas Baines who was the first to paint them during his expedition in 1862. Since this watercolour was done well over 140 years ago the scene has hardly changed except, sadly, for the growing amount of litter.

The seven giant trees dominate a small island on the edge of the open grassless Kudiakam Pan. They create an ideal picnic spot and always afford visitors respite in their deep, cool shade.

People often used to camp here, but now that this area has been incorporated in the national park this is no longer permitted, and it will be years before the area recovers from the damage of uncontrolled camping.

To get to Baines' Baobabs take the western turning at the Phuduhudu crossroads. After a short distance the road forks. Both routes lead to the baobabs, being wet and dry routes respectively.

At 11km (7 miles), the dry route, which veers to the right, is the shorter and more attractive of the two routes, taking you along Kudiakam Pan to the baobabs. If the ground is wet or if there has been recent rain take the left route, which goes for just over 13km (8 miles), before you will see the trees on the right. Take the right turn and go for a further 3.5km (2 miles) along this track until you reach the landmark.

Above: *Blue wildebeest gather in the grassy woodlands for their annual migration.*
Opposite: *Baines' Baobabs stand much as they did when the famous painter and naturalist Thomas Baines paid an historic visit to the area.*

WILDEBEEST ON THE MOVE

Blue wildebeest, which are now by no means the most common antelope in the area, were once plentiful. In 1980 the last huge migration of these animals, reminiscent of the vast Serengeti migrations, crossed the Makgadikgadi. Over 100,000 animals were involved and the herd was over 16km (10 miles) long and 10km (6 miles) wide.

Below: *A Kalahari tent tortoise, knee-high in water, illustrates the miniscule depth of the rain-filled pan.*

NXAI PAN ★★★

Unlike the salt pans which characterize the rest of the Makgadikgadi, Nxai Pan is covered with short sweet grass which provides good grazing and attracts large herds of springbok and impala. It is very unusual to see these two antelope species together on the same range and the only other place where this occurs to a significant degree is Etosha Pan in Namibia. Other game includes the desert-adapted gemsbok, giraffe, kudu, hartebeest, zebra, and the migratory wildebeest, as well as leopard, lion and hyena.

South Camp ★

There are two camp sites at Nxai Pan. South Camp is a short distance from the Scout Camp on the edge of Nxai. Take a right turn directly after entering the old gate; the camp is set in a grove of terminalia trees. There is an observation platform from which one can view game including (if you are lucky) leopard.

There is a remarkable array of birds to be seen in the Nxai Pan area, including the very common black korhaan, kestrels and goshawks, as well as the world's heaviest flying bird, the kori bustard which weighs in at nearly 40kg (88 lb).

North Camp ★

North Camp is at the top end of Nxai Pan, 8km (5 miles) from the old gate. It is set in a clearing in mopane woodland, but does not have a great deal of shade or a view of the pan. Both North and South camps have barbecue sites, running water and ablution blocks with flush toilets and shower facilities.

The Makgadikgadi Pans at a Glance

The southern Makgadikgadi and Nxai Pan Game Reserve, Ntwetwe and Sowa Pans are best for **game viewing** from **Apr–Jul**. In the Nxai Pan area, game viewing is best from **Dec–Apr**. In eastern Sowa, **water birds** can be seen between **Jan–Mar** depending on the rains and the flow of the Nata River. Roads can become impassible during the wet season (Dec–Mar). There can be violent **dust storms** in **October** and early **November**.

There are airstrips at Gweta and Nata. Four-wheel-drive is necessary in the park. Hitch-hiking is not advisable. There is a good tar road from Francistown and Maun. Vehicles can be hired from Maun and Francistown where there are larger airports. Access can be gained via Serowe and Orapa, but the tracks are rough. Walking is permitted in the reserve.

Four-wheel-drive is vital. Tell someone your itinerary so they can organize a search if you break down. Consider hiring a guide from a local village, especially if crossing remote areas.

LUXURY
Jack's Camp, tel: 686-0086, fax: 686-0632, e-mail: travelshop@ows.bw Exclusive tented camp.

San Camp, adjoining National Park. Contact Jack's Camp.

BUDGET
Nata Lodge, Francistown road, near Sowa Pan, tel: 621-1260. Between Nata and the Bird Sanctuary, with chalets, camping, restaurant and pool.
Sua Pan Lodge, in Nata village, tel: 621-1220. Offers chalets and camping.
Gweta Rest Camp, in Gweta village near Ntwetwe Pan, tel: 621-2220. Chalets, camp sites.
National park camp sites, book through Parks and Reserves. Reservations, tel: 318-0774, fax: 318-0775.

Francistown
LUXURY
Cresta Thapama Hotel & Casino, tel: 241-3872, fax: 241-3766, e-mail: resthapama@cresta.co.bw Luxury accommodation, restaurant and casino near the centre of Francistown.
MID-RANGE
The Marang, tel: 241-3991, fax: 241-2130, e-mail: resmarang@cresta.co.bw Excellent à la carte restaurant, luxury rooms, tree-top cabins and camping.

BUDGET
Tati River Lodge, tel: 240-6000, fax: 240-6080, e-mail: tri@info.bw Air-conditioned *en-suite* rooms, restaurant, pool, caravan and camp site.
Town Lodge, tel: 241-8802, fax: 241-8805, e-mail: jog@info.bw Exclusive accommodation and restaurant.

Visitors to Makgadikgadi must bring their own provisions and water. Supplies can be bought in Francistown, Maun, Nata and Gweta, but not at Orapa. There are good restaurants at the above hotels and lodges, but Jack's Camp and San Camp are not open to day visitors.

Guided safaris: safari operators offer horseback safaris, quad-bike excursions and sand windsurfing. If there is water on the pans canoeing and sailing are also possible. Jack's Camp and Gweta Rest Camp offer quad-bike safaris. Gweta Rest Camp and Nata Lodge organize horseback safaris. 'Sunset cruises' onto Sowa Pan are also offered from Nata Lodge.

NATA	J	F	M	A	M	J	J	A	S	O	N	D
MIN AVE TEMP. °C	19	18	17	14	9	6	5	8	12	16	18	19
MIN AVE TEMP. °F	66	64	63	57	48	43	41	46	54	61	64	66
MAX AVE TEMP. °C	31	30	30	28	26	23	23	26	30	31	31	31
MAX AVE TEMP. °F	88	86	86	82	79	73	73	79	86	88	88	88
RAINFALL mm	111	97	58	29	2	2	1	0	5	29	55	91
RAINFALL in	4.4	3.8	2.3	1.1	0.1	0.1	0	0	0.2	1.1	2.2	3.6

5
The Tuli Block and Eastern Botswana

The Kalahari sands don't quite reach the far eastern edge of Botswana and, with a higher average rainfall than elsewhere, this thin strip of land has the greatest agricultural potential in an otherwise barren country. Almost 80% of Botswana's population lives in this region, stretching from Ramokgwebana northeast of Francistown to Ramatlabama southwest of Lobatse. Between these points lie the urban centres of Gaborone, Mahalapye, Palapye, Selebi-Phikwe and Francistown, and the wildlife reserves of the Tuli Block.

THE TULI BLOCK

Set in a landscape of striking natural beauty in the extreme southeast of the country, the Tuli Block is a thin strip of commercial farmland which includes the largest privately owned game conservation area in southern Africa, combining an area of 120,000ha (300,000 acres) of game reserves, hunting and conservation areas.

The land was originally ceded to the British government by **Chief Khama III** of the Ngwato tribe in 1885. It was intended to establish a buffer zone to halt the Boer expansion and provide the British with a corridor in which to build their planned 'Cape to Cairo' railway line. However, the concession proved unsuitable for the railway, which was eventually built further to the west. The British finally transferred its administration to Cecil Rhodes' British South Africa Company (BSAC) which had colonized Rhodesia. In 1904, the BSAC divided the Tuli Block into lots which it sold to European farmers.

Opposite: *Mashatu boasts the largest elephant population on private land anywhere in the world.*

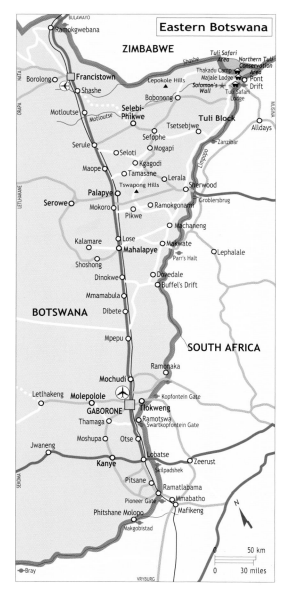

Over a period of time, as ownership of these farms began to consolidate and as government pressure increased for better utilization of the land, it became possible for private game reserves to be established. This led to the creation of the **North-East Tuli Game Reserve** which occupies the entire Tuli Block area north of the Motloutse River and is made up of several private reserves such as the Mashatu and Tuli game reserves.

MASHATU GAME RESERVE ★★★

Mashatu Game Reserve occupies the area between the Shashe and Limpopo rivers south of the Tuli Circle and covers 46,000ha (113,000 acres) of picturesque unspoilt countryside.

Over 350 bird species have been identified in the area and, with over 800 elephants, Mashatu boasts the largest **elephant** population on private land in the world. One of the reserve's attractions are the game viewing walks and night drives on offer. The latter are not permitted in Botswana's national parks, so many visitors miss seeing nocturnal predators such as leopard, lynx and wild cat, which are reasonably common sightings in Mashatu.

The River Confluence ★★★

The reserve is immense, usually taking more than a couple of days to explore. While in the area, visitors should try to arrange a trip to the confluence of the Shashe and Limpopo rivers where Botswana, South

Africa and Zimbabwe meet at the most easterly point of Botswana. This is an interesting area of riverine woodland and tall trees with plenty of elephant and other wildlife, while closer to the water's edge you are likely to see the colourful Meyer's parrot.

Above: *Guests enjoy a sumptuous breakfast after an early morning game drive in Mashatu.*

Majale and Thakadu ★★★

Majale offers luxury chalets for up to 30 guests with a thatched observation bar overlooking a floodlit water hole. Thakadu tented camp on the edge of the Tuli Circle is more rustic, but equally luxurious, with a similar thatched bar and game hide at the nearby water hole.

Routes into the Tuli Area

While the main roads into the Tuli area are generally gravel, they are quite good and most are easily negotiable in two-wheel-drive vehicles. There are several routes to Mashatu and Tuli Safari Lodge from Gaborone. You can turn left after the bridge on the outskirts of Mahalapye towards Makwate and the South African border post at Parr's Halt. This turning is rather incongruously signposted 'Flower Town', but is a well-maintained gravel road suitable for saloon cars. Parr's Halt is generally well signposted, but be sure to take the right-hand fork at the Machaneng turn-off.

THE TULI CIRCLE

South of Francistown the Zimbabwe/Botswana border is defined by the Shashe River, except for a unique semicircle of land called the Tuli Circle that juts into Botswana at the head of the Tuli Block. This piece of land was granted to the British South Africa Company in 1891 by Khama III to ensure that the outbreak of lung sickness did not infect the cattle at Fort Tuli. It is also interesting to note that the 16km (9 mile) radius of the circle is the exact range of the largest artillery gun stationed in the fort at the time!

Above: *Almost 1000 years ago the Tuli area was the centre of an empire. All that remains are numerous unexcavated ruins.*
Opposite: *The idyllic swimming pool at Tuli Safari Lodge.*

At Parr's Halt cross into South Africa from where the road becomes good tarmac. Just before reaching Ellisras, turn left to Swartwater and the road takes you via Alldays to Pont Drift.

At Pont Drift clear the South African Customs. If the Limpopo is dry, a vehicle will collect you from the car park and take you across the border back into Botswana. If the river is in flood you can cross it in the wire cage of the **Mashatu Cableway**. Confirm collection times when you make your bookings and remember that all the small border posts along the Limpopo close at 16:00, except for Martin's Drift which closes at 18:00. As an alternative you can take the route from Palapye to Martin's Drift and up to Pont Drift, which is about the same distance.

There is a good tar road from Selebi-Phikwe to Lekkerpoot, which is just 27km (17 miles) from the Zanzibar border post. This road is not only an easy access route into the Tuli area, but is also a popular short cut for road travellers driving up from Johannesburg, via Ellisras and Selebi-Phikwe, to the reserves in northern Botswana. The road from Lekkerpoot to Parr's Halt is gravel, but, with care, is easily navigable. Trucks are not permitted to use this road after 18:00.

Alternatively, from Gaborone follow the same route to Parr's Halt, but turn left 8km (5 miles) before the border post and drive via Sherwood Ranch, Zanzibar, Baines Drift and on to the signposted reserve entrance.

Another route is from Palapye to Martin's Drift where you can turn left and follow the Limpopo through Zanzibar and Baines Drift up to Pont Drift. The turn-offs to Mashatu and Tuli Safari Lodge are both just before Pont Drift after you cross the Motloutse River and the Talana Farms. From Bobonong there is also a very scenic four-wheel-drive route into Tuli via the villages of Mathlabaneng and Gubajongo.

Note: If you are not booked into any of the lodges or reserves you are not permitted to leave the main road or take any of the game-viewing routes in this area as it is private property.

TULI GAME RESERVE ★★★
Tuli Safari Lodge ★★★

Tuli Safari Lodge is the oldest of the lodges in the area and is situated on the 7500ha (18,500 acre) private reserve adjacent to Mashatu.

Unlike Mashatu, Tuli Safari Lodge allows children. There are three game hides in the reserve overlooking perennial water holes, and one of the hides offers accommodation for up to four guests.

Nokalodi Tented Camp ★★

In the southern end of Tuli Game Reserve, situated in riverine woodland on the Limpopo's banks, is Nokalodi tented camp. It is a small camp with just four palm-covered safari tents, and its intimacy has made it an attractive destination for small parties of self-catering guests.

Note: The route to Tuli Lodge is the same as the one to Mashatu.

SOLOMON'S WALL AND THE GRANITE HILLS
Solomon's Wall ★★★

Of all the many fascinating geological features in Botswana, Solomon's Wall in the Tuli Block is one of the most remarkable. This

THE RIVER OF DIAMONDS

The Motloutse River, (the name means 'Great Elephant') can trace its source to the west of Francistown. Eons ago, diamonds were carried along the river course, where they lay until the 1950s when the first diamonds in Botswana were discovered in the Motloutse's riverbed near Solomon's Wall. After 12 years of intensive prospecting these diamonds led to the discovery of the Orapa diamond pipe, the second-largest kimberlite pipe in the world.

FASCINATING FLORA

The flora of the North-East Tuli Game Reserve is quite remarkable with a variety of unusual trees and plants making their home here. The trees to be found include the strange paperbark tree (*Commiphora marlothii*); the largest acacia in southern Africa (*Acacia albida*), which grows to a height of 30m (100ft) and loses its leaves in summer; the fever tree which is mentioned in Rudyard Kipling's *Just So Stories*; and both the large- and small-leafed fig trees.

basalt dyke once formed a natural dam wall across the Motloutse River, and the two sides of this breached barrier still stand up to 30m (100ft) high, guarding each side of the narrow gorge.

The vertical sides of this ancient dyke held back a great lake behind what must have been a beautiful waterfall. Evidence of this lake is in the number of alluvial semiprecious stones that can be found in this area along the Motloutse's riverbed.

Four-wheel-drive is necessary to reach Solomon's Wall, but it is well worth visiting. There are often deep pools of water, and shade under the fever trees, but it is private property and you must have permission to visit the site.

In the Tuli area there are two ranges of granite hills which are of great historical and archaeological interest.

The Lepokole Hills ★★

The Lepokole Hills north of Bobonong are the southern-most extension of the Matopos Hills in Zimbabwe, and are made up of the same immense granite blocks, often piled high into tall castles of fissured rock.

It is in these hills that the last of the **San** in eastern Botswana took refuge from the encroaching 'civiliza-

Below: *The towering buttress of Solomon's Wall juts into the Motloutse riverbed.*

tion'. Their presence is recorded in the paintings found in the caves and rocky overhangs of the *kopjes*. In addition to the Bushman paintings, the Lepokole Hills also contain a wealth of archaeological treasures, from Stone Age tools and ancient pottery to stone walls and mud granaries all left by long-forgotten people.

Visitors to the Lepokole Hills must be completely self-sufficient as only basic supplies can be obtained in Bobonong. From the village a rough four-wheel-drive track leads visitors for 15km (9 miles) into the hills. There are no public camp sites or facilities in the hills and if one wants to camp in the area it is a courtesy to ask permission from the *kgosi* (chief) in Bobonong.

Tswapong Hills **

For the more adventurous, a true journey of discovery awaits those

who set out to explore the Tswapong Hills east of Palapye. This is probably one of the least known areas of Botswana, yet it is less than 50km (30 miles) off the main Gaborone/Francistown highway.

The shear-sided hills are made up of compressed layers of sandstone, shales and quartzites, giving them their distinctive colours

It is, however, the water which is Tswapong's unique attraction. In this thirsty country, deep gorges have been carved into the hills giving rise to seasonal rivers, fed by natural springs where absorbed rain flows out of the porous rock. In places, these springs give rise to streams forming waterfalls with deep moss-edged pools.

Several waterfalls can be found near the village of Moremi, while a large colony of **Cape vultures** is established in the cliffs near the village of Gootau. Before visiting either of these sites, be sure to ask permission from the village chiefs.

With the abundant water in these scenic hills comes a diversity of flora and fauna and almost half of Botswana's 250 butterfly species can be found here. **Butterflies** are particularly plentiful near Moeng College, Botswana's first secondary school.

Above: *The closest relative to the inquisitive dassie is the elephant.*

THE DASSIE'S TAIL

Dassies can often be seen sunning themselves on rocks and boulders. Batswana folklore states that in the beginning when God decided to give all the animals tails, the dassie did not receive his and was very sad at having been left out. The other animals felt so sorry for him that they told him to wait out on the rocky hilltops so that when God came back he would see the dassie first and would give him a tail of his own. So next time you see a dassie sitting out on a ledge scanning the sky, remember who he might be waiting for.

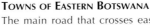

Opposite: *The shepherd's tree is an important source of nutrition.*
Below: *Safety is vital at the BCL copper and nickle mine in Selebi-Phikwe.*

TOWNS OF EASTERN BOTSWANA

The main road that crosses eastern Botswana linking Gaborone and Francistown is a double-lane tarred road.

The **Tropic of Capricorn** crosses this road 152km (91 miles) north of Gaborone. At this point a dirt road turns off to the east to the now closed border post of Buffel's Drift on the Limpopo River. From here there is a four-wheel-drive track north along the riverbank to the southern end of the Tuli Block farms. There is a gate to the private farmlands, but traffic is permitted to those staying at the private camps or lodges along the river in this area.

Mahalapye ★

The town of Mahalapye lies just within the tropics, 198km (119 miles) from Gaborone. It is a busy, dusty little metropolis with numerous shops, garages, takeaways and stores lining the road as it meanders between the riverbed and the rocky *kopjes* that hem in the town. In the early 1990s the town grew considerably with the establishment of the Botswana Railways Headquarters here.

Shoshong ★

Just 30km (18 miles) west of Mahalapye is the historical village of Shoshong, once the old Ngwato capital from where Chief Khama gave permission to the ill-fated 'Thirstland Trekkers' to cross his territory in the late 1870s. It was here that **John Mackenzie** established a

mission station where he lived for 14 years, during which time he played a crucial role in helping the chiefs secure British protection and halt the feared Boer expansion. The remains of his church can still be seen here, as well as the large flat 'church bell' stone which, when struck by another rock, resonated like a bell to hail the people to church.

Palapye ★

About 70km (42 miles) beyond Mahalapye is the crossroads to Serowe (see page 82) and Palapye where considerable coal deposits have been discovered. The main town of Palapye is a short distance east of the main road. Petrol is available here. Palapye is considered to be the powerhouse of Botswana; it is home to the Morupule power station, which supplies most of the country's needs. The original names of Mahalapye and Palapye are very similar, being Mhalatswe and Phalatswe respectively. Both refer to the impala antelope (Aepyceros melampus) which used to thrive in the area.

Selebi-Phikwe ★

Beyond Palapye the main road passes through stands of mopane woodland before reaching the eastern turn-off to the mining town of Selebi-Phikwe 88km (53 miles) southwest of Francistown. Many visitors to Botswana in the past have missed this town, located just over 50km (33 miles) off the main road, but it has grown into the third-largest urban centre in Botswana. With the completion of the tarred road from the Martin's Drift border post, Selebi-Phikwe is now a convenient halfway stopover between Johannesburg (via Ellisras) and Botswana's northern tourist attractions.

Originally there were two tiny places called Selebi and Phikwe, which straddled a large undiscovered deposit of copper and nickel in the area. When the mineral wealth of the area was discovered in the 1960s a mine and township was built in the woodland between the places with the combined name of Selebi-Phikwe.

The mining operations at Selebi-Phikwe have not been as successful as expected and the economy of the area has diversified into areas such as textiles, manufacturing and commerce. A power grid terminal was opened here in 1996 to carry electricity from South Africa through to Zimbabwe – the first stage of the Southern African Power Pool.

THE SMELLY SHEPHERD'S TREE

The shepherd's tree (Boscia albitrunca) occurs throughout Botswana and is known as the 'tree of life', being an immensely important source of nutrition for both animals and humans. Its leaves have a high vitamin A content, the hollow trunks form natural reservoirs and the roots can be eaten raw or cooked, or can be roasted and ground into a satisfying coffee substitute. The roots also have preservative properties.The shepherd's tree flowers in spring after the first rains, with a profusion of small sweet-smelling yellow flowers. But be warned there is a sub-species called the smelly shepherd's tree (Boscia foetida) which is common in the Tuli area and, for all its virtues, when in flower it smells worse than a public toilet.

The Tuli Block and Eastern Botswana at a Glance

BEST TIMES TO VISIT

Game viewing in this corner of Botswana is best from **April** to **December** when the animals congregate around the permanent water points. While the summer months from October to April can be extremely hot, and even during the winter, the day temperature can often reach as high as 35°C (95°F) while the nights are very cold.

GETTING THERE

There is a regional airport at **Selebi-Phikwe** which is serviced by charter flights, but to reach the tourist areas of the Tuli Block one must fly into the landing strip which is operated by Tuli Safari Lodge in the northern Tuli Block. There are no scheduled Air Botswana flights into Tuli, but there are regular charter flights which can be organized from any major centre in or outside Botswana. Flying time is about one and a half hours from Gaborone, Johannesburg or Harare. Customs and Immigration facilities are available at this landing strip for tourists flying into the area from outside Botswana.
By road there are several two-wheel- and four-wheel-drive routes. From Johannesburg, drive to the Pont Drift border post via Ellisras and Alldays. From Zimbabwe, visitors can either cross into Botswana via Plumtree and Francistown or go through Beit Bridge and

approach Pont Drift via Musina. From Gaborone one can drive via Mahalapye and cross the Parr's Halt border post, though it is also possible to go via Palapye, or to turn right (east) at the Tropic of Capricorn and drive to Buffel's Drift on the Limpopo where you turn left (north) and enter the bottom end of the Tuli Block (four-wheel-drive is recommended for this route). From Francistown one can reach the Tuli Block either via Selebi-Phikwe or Palapye. Note that the Buffel's Drift border post has been closed for years and the other border posts across the Limpopo River are only open from 08:00–16:00.

GETTING AROUND

As most of the Tuli area is private property travellers who are not booked into any of the lodges or camps cannot conduct their own game drives, save for sticking to the main road through the area and hoping for the best. But almost all of the private reserves offer their guests excellent guided day and night game drives as well as guided walks.

WHERE TO STAY

As the contact numbers of the following establishments are subject to change, if you are having trouble contacting either their local or Johannesburg (with the prefix +27 11) numbers try any of the established travel agents such as:

Harvey World Travel, tel: 390-4360, fax: 390-5840.
Kudu Travel, tel: 397-2224, fax: 397-4224, e-mail: nevilles.kudu@galileosa.co.za
SAA City Centre – The Travelling Company on tel: 395-2021, fax: 390-5552.
Travelwise on tel: 390-3244, fax: 390-3245.

Tuli

LUXURY

Mashatu Game Reserve, tel: 264-5321. Superb accommodation in the largest private game reserve in southern Africa at **Majale Lodge** or the tented **Thakadu Camp**. Small children not permitted.
Tuli Safari Lodge, tel: 264-5303. Luxury accommodation with several excellent drives and walks. Guests can also overnight at the game hide.

BUDGET

Jwala Game Lodge, tel: (+27 11) 886-8383, fax: (+27 11) 886-7892. North of the Tuli Circle, this reserve offers a beautifully decorated self-catering lodge and two tented bush camps offering game drives and walks.
Limpopo River Lodge, tel: 391-2280, e-mail: van&truck hire@mega.bw Situated at the southern end of the Tuli Block with a swimming pool and self-catering chalets right on the river's edge. Access is via the Tropic of Capricorn turning, off the main Gaborone/ Francistown road.

The Tuli Block and Eastern Botswana at a Glance

Nokalodi Tented Camp, tel: (+27 11) 474-3453, fax: (+27 11) 474-8563. Located near Tuli Safari Lodge. The tariff for the self-catering tented accommodation includes drives and walks.

Mawana Nature Reserve, tel: (+ 27 11) 706-2668. Offers self-catering accommodation in five double tents set under the trees at Koro Bush Camp on the banks of the Limpopo River.

Stevensford Game Reserve, tel: 395-2788, fax: 395-2757. One of the oldest and longest established reserves in the Tuli area.

Talana Farms, tel: 264-5310. Four self-catering chalets set under the shady trees, situated just to the south of the Motloutse River.

Mahalapye
Budget

Mahalapye Hotel, tel: 471-0200. Accommodation with bar, restaurant and swimming pool overlooking the generally dry river bed.

Oasis Lodge, tel: 471-2081, fax: 471-2082. Part of the Oasis chain.

Palapye
Mid-range

Cresta Botsalo Hotel, tel: 492-0245, fax: 492-0587, e-mail: resbotsalo@cresta. co.bw Comfortable facilities with good restaurant and swimming pool, situated right on the main road.

Budget

Horizon Holiday Lodges, tel: 492-4391.

Palapye Hotel, tel: 492-0277. Accommodation with restaurant and bar.

Selebi-Phikwe
Mid-range

Cresta Bosele Hotel, tel: 261-0675, fax: 261-1083, e-mail: resbosele@cresta. co.bw Centrally located, comfortable, full-service hotel and casino with good restaurant and the vibrant Menateng Casino.

Budget

Syringa Lodge & Spur, tel: 261-0444, fax: 261-0450, e-mail: syringap@ syringa.co.bw Reasonably priced accommodation on the airport road with popular Spur family restaurant as well as car-hire facilities.

WHERE TO EAT

The lodges and camps in the Tuli Block are not open to casual visitors, but there are restaurants at all the hotels in the main centres in eastern Botswana as well as cafés and takeaways.

Mahalapye
Kaytees Restaurant, tel: 471-0795. Situated on the main road, Kaytees restaurant is great for a takeaway breakfast.

Palapye
Riverside Restaurant, tel: 492-0641. This restaurant offers good value for money, traditional fare.

Selebi-Phikwe
Giavanos Restaurant, tel: 261-5999. Sit-down and takeaway Italian and pizzas. **Grill Master**, tel: 261-4300. Steakhouse.

TOURS AND EXCURSIONS

Generally independent tour operators do not organize excursions into the Tuli area, but all travel agents can arrange all-inclusive or self-catering trips to any of the lodges or camps in the area, tailored to match any particular budget.

USEFUL CONTACTS

Kalahari Air Services for charters into the Tuli area; tel: 395-1804, fax: 391-2015, e-mail: kasac@info.bw

BOBONONG	J	F	M	A	M	J	J	A	S	O	N	D
MIN AVE TEMP. °C	20	19	17	14	8	5	4	8	12	16	18	19
MIN AVE TEMP. °F	68	66	63	57	46	41	39	46	54	61	64	66
MAX AVE TEMP. °C	32	31	30	27	25	22	22	25	29	30	31	31
MAX AVE TEMP. °F	90	88	86	81	77	72	72	77	84	86	88	88
RAINFALL mm	71	80	32	28	4	3	0	0	4	25	38	63
RAINFALL in	2.8	3.2	1.3	1.1	0.2	0.1	0	0	0.2	1	1.9	2.5

6
The Central Kalahari

In the middle of Botswana lies the heart of the Kalahari – a flat sea of sand in a dry and featureless world. But within this monotony a wealth of wildlife and breathtaking landscapes awaits discovery.

The shimmering façade of baked sand hides an incredible diversity of strangely adapted plant and animal life. There is the Devil's claw, a spiky weed pod that contains natural aspirin; the majestic gemsbok with a built-in air conditioner; and the distasteful dung beetle upon whom almost everyone's survival depends.

This expansive landscape has always held a magnetic attraction for man, and since the middle of the 19th century explorers have been drawn here, searching for undiscovered wealth. So far treasure and lost cities have eluded all, and many people have died trying to cross the dry interior. A rusty trail of broken, sun-bleached wagons can still be found littering the lost Missionaries' Road which once carved its way across this inhospitable interior, bringing with it the first early explorers.

THE CENTRAL KALAHARI GAME RESERVE ★★★
Established in 1961 this massive reserve covers 52,800km² (20,000 sq miles), just slightly smaller than the combined size of Holland and Belgium.

But, unlike other reserves which are usually set aside to protect animals, this area was originally intended as a sanctuary for its human inhabitants – it was the last domain of the nomadic Bushmen. Until recently there were still a few small groups of these

DON'T MISS

★★★ **Cheetah** at the kill.
★★ The **vast openness** of wide game-filled plains.
★ The **lion's roar** echoing against the black star-studded night sky.
★ Following in the Owens' footsteps across the dry **Deception Pan**.

Opposite: *The setting sun casts a crimson glow over the Kalahari landscape.*

CLIMATE

The short spring and autumn seasons from September to October and from April to May respectively are the best times to visit when it is neither too hot nor too cold. The temperatures can become unbearable in the summer months from November to March with day temperatures often exceeding 40°C (104°F), broken by occasional and violent thunderstorms. In winter the nights are bitterly cold with temperatures having been known to drop as low as -10°C (14°F)!

remarkable Stone Age people wandering through the wastes of the southern reserve, completely unaware of the encroaching 'civilized' world.

The last of these Bushmen, or San as they are known, now reside in small village communities in the reserve at places like Xade, Xaka, Molapo and Metseamonong.

Deception Valley ★★★

Deception Valley is all that remains of a sprawling riverbed that has long since dried up. Stretching across about 80km (48 miles) of the park's north, the valley is now covered with short grass, dotted with the occasional island of bushy trees. Some of the roots of the larger trees extend as far as 50m (165ft) below the surface to the water table, enabling them to survive the dry winters.

The low canopies of these tree grove islands, usually made up of **umbrella thorn** (*Acacia tortilis*) and **buffalo thorn** (*Ziziphus mucronata*) provide shelter for game during the heat of the day and one can often see lion dozing in the shade of these thickets.

The fossil valley was first brought to the world's attention in 1985, by the book *Cry of the Kalahari* written by Mark and Delia Owens, who lived on the pan for seven years studying the **brown hyena** that live here.

Camping is permitted in Deception Valley at Piper's Pan and at Sunday Pan, although there is **no drinking water** or any other facilities at these sites. Drinking water is only available in the reserve at the **Game Scout Camp** at Matswere,

Central Kalahari

WARNING: DEADLY GRASS

There are very real dangers awaiting the unwary traveller in the Kalahari. With the abundance of dry grass the conditions are unique and complacency could lead to tragedy in an area where the next passing vehicle could be many days or even months away.

• **Burning seeds:** With the low volumes of traffic the grass in the middle of the tracks can grow very tall and after rain it is heavy with long, black grass seeds. These can accumulate in crevices under the vehicle, packing into a solid mass particularly around the exposed exhaust area. Within minutes this flammable matrix can start to smoulder. When the car slows down or stops the woody material is engulfed in flames. If the area is grassy with telltale dark tasselled seeds, check under the vehicle every five minutes or so, clearing them away every time. It's also worth tying an old sack onto the engine grill to drag under the vehicle; this helps to disperse the seeds. If you are faced with a fire save your water, as that will be vital for surviving the following days waiting for help to arrive. Use a fire extinguisher if you have one, if not, try to smother the flames with the sand under the car and pinch any ruptured fuel lines to stop the fire from spreading.

• **Radiator damage:** Thousands of seeds can clog up radiator vents reducing efficiency and causing overheating. To protect against this, cover the radiator with a fine wire mesh to catch the seeds, and clear the mesh regularly. If the radiator does get clogged up the only thing to do is to clear it, and this often involves laborious hours of picking individual seeds out with a needle.

• **Burning grass:** There is a danger of a hot exhaust igniting grass under the vehicle. To avoid this do not pull off the road or stop in tall grass for any reason. If you want to stop, stop in the middle of the road where no grass will be in contact with the exhaust system. (In any case, driving off the road is prohibited in the national parks and permanently scars the fragile vegetation.)

near to the entrance gate on the road from Rakops. It is important to note that **firewood** must also be brought along as any removal of wood or even kindling will permanently damage the fragile desert environment.

Routes into the Central Kalahari Game Reserve

There are several routes into the reserve; the most well used is via **Rakops**. **From Gaborone** the best route to Rakops is to drive from Palapye to Serowe, on to the villages of Paje and Mmashoro. From Mmashoro travel on past Letlhakane and the closed diamond-mining town of Orapa to Mopipi, which is 281km (170 miles) from Serowe. From Mopipi it is another 74km (45 miles) to Rakops.

At the western edge of Rakops village is a dirt road signposted to the Central Kalahari Game Reserve, and 55km (33 miles) down this road is the park entrance. Although the road is reasonably well maintained, four-wheel-drive is recommended.

Below: *The golden perennial grasses of the Kalahari stabilize the ancient fossil dunes.*

From Francistown take the Orapa road, skirting the southern side of the Orapa Mine Concession to join up with the Mopipi road and on to Rakops.

The road **from Maun** to the Central Kalahari Game Reserve (CKGR) has been upgraded, making the journey a lot quicker and easier. You can take the dirt turn-off to Makalamabedi and link through to Motopi and work your way down the cordon fence. The recommended route, however, is to go about 105km (63 miles) from Maun and just before the Bushman's pits turn south to the village of Matima where you join the new road that skirts the Makgadikgadi and Nxai Pan National Park down to Rakops.

The route **from Ghanzi** is definitely for the adventurous. Take the road to Tswaane, then after 27km (17 miles) turn to the east on a very challenging track to the San village of Xade which is 160km (96 miles) away. From Xade take the northern track to Piper Pans which are 79km (48 miles) to the north. From Pipers, Deception Pan is another 80km (48 miles) northeast.

As most visitors to the CKGR drive in via Serowe it is worth exploring this scenic and historic village.

SEROWE

Set in rocky hills 47km (28 miles) west of Palapye, Serowe is the capital of the Bangwato tribe, the largest of Botswana's Tswana tribes. With a population of over 50,000 people, this attractively located settlement is reputed to be the largest traditional tribal village in Africa. It is also the birthplace of the country's first president, Sir Seretse Khama, who is buried with other important members of the royal house, including King Khama III at the summit of **Thathaganyane Hill**. It is worth visiting the cemetery to appreciate the wonderful view, but you will need a police escort to climb the hill.

Khama III Memorial Museum ★

At the base of the hill is the Khama III Memorial Museum which occupies the 'Red House' built especially for this celebrated chief in 1910. The museum, in addition to natural history displays, commemorates the Ngwato and San culture and history.

Serowe was also home to the well-known South African novelist **Bessie Head** who wrote numerous books including *Serowe: Village of the Rain Wind* based on local village life. Many of her letters and manuscripts are preserved in the museum.

There are several petrol stations and a choice of shops and supermarkets, making Serowe a convenient supply stop for travellers venturing into the Central Kalahari.

SACRED DUIKER

The **Bangwato** tribe hold the small duiker antelope sacred. It was adopted as their totem animal as, according to legend, a duiker saved the life of the Bangwato's founding chief by distracting his enemy at a crucial moment. A bronze duiker created by the famous South African sculptor **Anton van Wouw** now graces the grave of Khama III at the Royal Cemetery in Serowe.

The Khama Rhino Sanctuary ★

In the early 1990s the people of Serowe proposed that a small game reserve be established at Serowe Pan north of the town on the Orapa road. This lead to the establishment of the Khama Rhino Sanctuary in 1993, with Paramount Chief of the Bangwato and Vice President of Botswana, Ian Khama as its patron.

This 4,300ha (10,625 acre) game reserve on tribal land is intended to provide a safe environment for the re-establishment of both black and white rhino populations. The last few wild black rhino in Botswana were transferred from Chobe to the Sanctuary in 1996, by which time it is believed that all the rest in the wild had been killed by poachers. The rhino share the reserve with a variety of indigenous game including red hartebeest, ostrich, brown hyena, leopard, jackal, steenbok, duiker, bat-eared fox, lynx and wildcat. The sanctuary is open daily and a nominal entrance fee is charged.

Opposite: *Traditional crafts are displayed in the Khama 'Red House' Museum in Serowe.*
Below: *Translocated rhino settle into their well-guarded new home at the Khama Rhino Sanctuary.*

KHUTSE GAME RESERVE ★★★

Although large by normal standards, Khutse Game Reserve, covering 2590km² (985 sq miles), is dwarfed

THE DEVIL'S CLAW

The **wild grapple** (*Harpago-phytum procumbens*), which grows in the remote Kalahari sands is locally know as Devil's claw due to its hard spiny pods which hook and stab into almost anything. These plants are one of Botswana's most effective traditional medicines. The plant contains **natural aspirin** and, while it has been used in Africa for centuries, modern scientists are only now recognizing it as being as effective as synthetic drugs in the treatment of a range of ailments including rheumatism, hypertension, gastrointestinal and skin problems, diabetes, neuralgia and arteriosclerosis. Tests have proven that grapple healed at least 60% of arthritis cases. While in Botswana be sure to try Devil's claw and your holiday could result in improved health.

by its vast neighbour, the Central Kalahari Game Reserve, with whom it shares its long northern boundary. Due to its proximity to Gaborone it is a popular weekend destination for people living in the capital. One of the greatest attractions of the park is the true peace and quiet that visitors find in the Kalahari.

Khutse, dotted with more than 60 seasonal pans, consists of wide open savanna plains of dry grassland with a sparse covering of thorn trees. Here, visitors are likely to see the three big cats: cheetah, leopard and lion. The open plains are ideal for cheetah, as they need the long runways to reach their phenomenal speeds of up to 120kph (75mph) to run down their prey.

Camp Sites

There is an established camp site with ablution blocks and running water at the entrance gate where park entry fees have to be paid. At the other 20 camp sites within the reserve there are, at most, only pit latrines and certainly no running water, so be sure to fill up at this main camp. The water here is unfortunately rather brackish. **Khutse Camp Site** is 13km (8 miles) from the entrance gate and is situated between a couple of open pans at the junction of the large loop road around the park.

The Pans

Golalabodimo Pan is right at the park gate. Almost directly after this pan is a turn-off to the north. This goes to the distant village of Gope in the Central Kalahari Game Reserve and should not be taken.

Going northwest the road passes **Motailane Pan** which has a water hole. This is followed by **Tshilwane Pan** bordering the Central Kalahari Game Reserve. The third pan, popular for its game concentrations, is **Mahurushele Pan** and there are a couple of camp sites near its edge. Close by is a camp site under a shady camel thorn tree near **Sekushuwe Pan**, while 11km (7 miles) further north at **Khankhe Pan** is a very attractive camp site on the sand dune overlooking the pan.

Left: *The magnificent leopard which, weight for weight, is the strongest of the world's cats.*
Opposite: *A grassy pan, damp from a local bore-hole, is one of the few sources of permanent water for the wildlife in Khutse.*

Khankhe Pan is actually within the Central Kalahari Game Reserve so do not drive further north from Khankhe Pan; the track heads off a great distance into the arid semidesert and should you get lost or break down help will be a long way away. Take the loop road that heads back in a southerly direction through open grassland for almost 30km (18 miles) before reaching the three camp sites at **Molose water hole**.

Note: camping is not permitted near this water hole as it disturbs the animals' access to the water.

Molose Pan has a distinctive sand dune overlooking its western edge and is the most reliable supply of drinking water in the reserve so considerable concentrations of game are often to be found here.

Further to the south is **Moreswe Pan**, with more camp sites equipped with pit latrines. This is probably the most popular camping area in the whole park with its reputation for concentrations of game and tall, attractive trees.

There is another water hole here, but its water is extremely saline and undrinkable except when it is diluted by rain water. Even so, many animals visit this borehole for the salt and minerals that they derive from both the water and the pan surface. In fact, the holes in the pan surface near the reservoir have been dug by gemsbok who, along with various animals, actually eat the mineral-rich soil. Be sure to look out for cheetah which are often sighted around Moreswe Pan.

THE LAST GREAT PLAIN

Unfortunately the delicate ecosystem of the Central Kalahari is at risk and soon will change or even disappear altogether. Since the 1980s animal populations have fallen dramatically with wildebeest and hartebeest numbers now less than 15% of what they were just a few decades ago. Hopefully, through the realization of its money-earning potential and the lobbying of the environmentally conscious international community, this last vestige of wild Africa will be protected for future generations.

PANS OF THE PAST

The pans in Khutse are relics of the superlake that once covered northern Botswana. The geology of this area began to take shape after the glaciation of Antarctica five million years ago, when southern Africa became drier. Easterly winds built up long sand dunes across the sub-continent which, when wetter times returned, channelled water into the superlake. The Meratswe River Valley which passes through Khutse was one of these channels which linked up with Lake Xau and on to the Makgadikgadi. It is believed that this river carried a great deal of water north-wards about 15,000 years ago, but with tectonic warp-ing of this lower end of the Great East African Rift Valley the flow of water was stopped and it dried up leaving the pans dotted across Khutse's shallow valley floor.

Remember that it is **forbidden** to drive across any of the pans and, if you do – even if you follow existing tracks across these fragile features – you will be asked to leave the park, as this causes irreparable damage. While you can walk across the pans, the Department of Wildlife and National Parks cannot be held responsible for your safety!

Routes into Khutse Game Reserve

The only practical route to Khutse Game Reserve is from Gaborone via Molepolole. Molepolole, which is 50km (30 miles) north of the Capital, is the last major village on the way to Khutse. From here take the tar road a further 65km (40 miles) to Letlhakeng. There is a small petrol station at Letlhakeng, but the tar ends here and from here on four-wheel-drive is very necessary.

Although Letlhakeng marks the start of the dry Kalahari sands, not so long ago this area was reputed to be lush. Several strong freshwater springs attracted large numbers of rhino, elephant and buffalo and, as a legacy of this now long-forgotten past, the name Letlhakeng means 'place of reeds'. From here it is a fur-ther 120km (72 miles) to the Khutse Game Scout Camp on a poorly signposted road via the tiny villages of Khudumelapye and Salajwe, after which the road becomes very sandy and difficult to negotiate.

At times the wide sand road is crisscrossed by a maze of secondary tracks and diversions, some leading off to cattleposts and others just routes around sandy patches. Always stick to the most well-used track as it is most likely to be the right one. The 240km (144 mile) journey from Gaborone will take five to six hours.

Almost at the entrance to Khutse Game Reserve is a small San settlement where crafts can be bought. Be considerate of these people's privacy and do not wander uninvited into their camp or take photographs without hav-ing at least asked permission.

Below: *The rolling grass-lands of the Central Kalahari stretch far beyond the horizon.*

The Central Kalahari at a Glance

BEST TIMES TO VISIT

The spring months of **September** and **October** and the autumn months of **April** and **May** are the most comfortable months to visit when it is neither too hot nor too cold. **Game viewing** is excellent in Khutse from **July** to **September** when large herds congregate around the pans. Deception Valley in the Central Kalahari Game Reserve is usually comfortable all year round. While generally good, the **game viewing** in the Central Kalahari is best after the **first rains** (**December/January**) when the landscape is transformed into a lush green parkland. Khutse can get crowded over long weekends, particularly Easter when people from Gaborone tend to visit.

GETTING THERE

It is not practical to fly into the Central Kalahari as you need to have vehicles on the ground. The best route into CKGR is therefore via **Rakops** from Gaborone or Francistown and from Matima if you are coming from Maun. Kutse is best approached via Molepolole.

GETTING AROUND

The choice is to hire a car, join a package tour or to use your own 4x4 vehicle. Car hire can be arranged through either **Avis**, tel: 397-5469, fax: 391-2205, e-mail : botswanares@avis.co.za **Budget**, tel: 390-2030, fax: 390-2028, e-mail:

Botswana@budget.co.za **Imperial**, tel: 390-7233, fax: 390-4460, or **Smart Car Rentals**, tel: 316-1116, fax: 316-1115.

WHERE TO STAY

There are no lodges or hotels in the Central Kalahari and one can only camp at designated camp sites. Other options are: **Boteti Hotel**, Letlhakane, tel: 297-8289, fax: 297-8251. Reasonable accommodation. **Mikelele Car Motel**, Letlhakane, tel: 297-8594. Overnight motel accommodation. **Lentswe Lodge**, Serowe, tel: 463-4333. **Serowe Hotel**, tel: 463-0234, fax: 463-0203. Budget accommodation with restaurant. **Tshwaragano Hotel**, Serowe, tel: 463-0377, fax: 463-1700. Inexpensive rondavels. **Khama Rhino Sanctuary**, tel: 463-0713, fax: 463-5808, e-mail: krst@botsnet.bw web: www.khamarhinosanctuary.org *En-suite* chalets and camp sites with excellent ablutions.

WHERE TO EAT

Apart from a few traditional restaurants and takeaways in Serowe and Letlhakane (such

as the Highway Filling Station and Restaurant) there are no other places to eat in the Central Kalahari and visitors must be self-sufficient, in terms of food and drinking water.

TOURS AND EXCURSIONS

There are no regular excursions into the Central Kalahari, but tailored trips can be organized through any reputable travel agent in Botswana, such as: **KOY Travel and Tours**, tel: 393-9602, fax: 393-9603, e-mail: sales@koytravel.com **Magic Travel and Tours**, tel: 397-4034, fax: 397-4041, e-mail: magictravel@botsnet.bw **Skylink Travel**, tel: 316-2599, fax: 316-3023, e-mail: anujj.skylink@galileosa.co.za

WHAT TO TAKE

In the Central Kalahari water and fuel are vital as there are no supplies anywhere. From the middle of the reserve the nearest town of any size is over 300km (185 miles) away in any direction! Take at least 5 litres (9 pints) of water per person per day, plus an extra 20% in case of emergency. Due to the fragile environment also please bring in all your own firewood.

KALAHARI	J	F	M	A	M	J	J	A	S	O	N	D
MIN AVE TEMP. °C	19	19	17	13	8	5	5	7	12	16	18	19
MIN AVE TEMP. °F	66	66	63	55	46	41	41	45	54	61	64	66
MAX AVE TEMP. °C	33	32	31	39	27	24	24	27	31	33	33	33
MAX AVE TEMP. °F	91	90	88	84	81	75	75	81	88	91	91	91
RAINFALL mm	102	77	57	33	7	1	0	1	5	22	47	72
RAINFALL in	4	3	2.2	1.3	0.3	0	0	0	0.2	0.9	1.9	2.8

7
Chobe National Park

Established in 1968 and covering 11,700km² (4450 sq miles), this vast northern park, named after the Chobe River, encompasses a variety of diverse habitats which are home to the greatest concentration of game on the southern African subcontinent.

From the dense riverine forests and swamplands of Chobe and Linyanti, towards the eastern Nogatsaa region, the countryside changes first to mopane and mixed deciduous forest, and then to open grassy plains and rocky *kopje* outcrops at Savuti in the southwest. Due to the seasonal availability of water across this vast terrain, Chobe is the site of a dramatic annual zebra migration. At this time the roads become almost impassable, congested with tens of thousands of animals forming a solid mass moving across the landscape.

Throughout the year herds of elephant and buffalo can be seen drinking along the river's edge, their numbers swelling into the hundreds and sometimes thousands during the dry season.

The park has four distinct areas: the **Chobe River frontage** including **Serondela**; the central area around **Nogatsaa** and the associated pans, which attract great concentrations of wildlife long into the dry season; **Linyanti** with its riverine marshes and papyrus beds; and the **Savuti** area which includes the Mababe Depression.

The most commonly used route into the park is via Kasane, near the Kazungula border post where the four countries of Botswana, Namibia, Zimbabwe and Zambia meet at a single point.

DON'T MISS

★★★ Watching the sunset from a **river barge**.
★★ Catching the fighting **tigerfish** in the Chobe.
★★ Finding **cheetah** at the kill in Savuti's grasslands.
★★ Being surrounded by thousands of **migrating zebra**.
★★ Spotting the rare **Chobe bushbuck** in riverine forest.
★★ Drifting past hippo grazing on **Sedudu Island**.
★ A day trip to the awesome **Victoria Falls**.

Opposite: *The wide, slow-moving Chobe River defines the edge of the national park.*

KASANE ★★

This scenic little town just east of the national park entrance gate is strung out along a shady tree-lined avenue on the Chobe river bank and is 12km (7 miles) west of Kazungula at the end of the main highway.

The boundary of the Chobe National Park butts right up to the western edge of the town and, as it is unfenced, many animals including elephant and hippo can be seen wandering casually through the streets and camp sites of Kasane.

There are several shops, garages, banks and river lodges in the village, which is also serviced by one of Botswana's few international airports, just some 4km (2.5 miles) from the town centre.

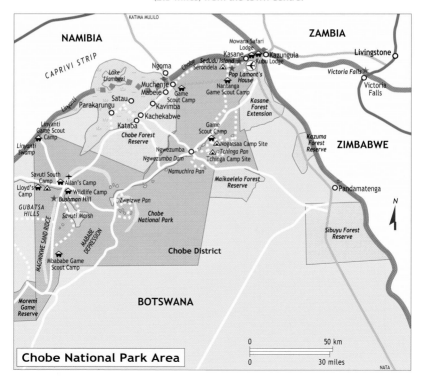

Chobe National Park Area

The crumpled remains of an ancient and once huge baobab tree (*Adansonia digitata*) can be seen from the main road in the police station grounds. The trunk is hollow and the tree was used as the local jail for many years before the current brick structure behind it was built.

Mowana Safari Lodge ★★★

Mowana Safari Lodge is situated a short distance out of Kasane on the Kazungula road, overlooking an attractive bend in the Chobe River near the Kasane Rapids. It is at this point that the river flows across a pronounced seam of basalt rock, speeding it on its way towards the awaiting Zambezi.

There are several natural picnic sites in this area and it is well worth a visit, particularly as a wealth of bird life can be seen along these rapids including several unusual species such as the **African finfoot** and the **halfcollared kingfisher**. There is a rough gravel track that leads down towards the river next to the large baobab tree at the entrance to Mowana Safari Lodge.

Mowana Safari Lodge overlooks the river in a beautiful setting; its remarkable architecture is built around an 800-year-old baobab tree.

Sedudu Island ★★★

The large flat grassy expanse of Sedudu Island fills the central channel of the Chobe River opposite Kasane. This island has always been contested between Namibia and Botswana, and is reputed to have been the site of the first shots of World War I fired between the Germans and the British. The debate was eventually resolved in 2000 with Sedudu being confirmed as part of Botswana after an international court studied the riverbed to determine exactly where the boundary ran. This has been an important decision as it is now part of the national park and is a vital grazing site for countless buffalo and elephant.

A FISHERMAN'S PARADISE

Having remained undiscovered for a long time, the Chobe River is now rapidly becoming an extremely popular fishing destination with over 90 different species of fish to be found in the wide waterways off Kasane. Over 20 of these varieties are popular table or sport fish, such as bream and the fighting tigerfish, and fully organized fishing safaris or private boat and tackle hire can be easily arranged at any of the lodges in Kasane or Kazungula.

Below: *Mowana Safari Lodge dominates the Chobe river bank.*

'POP' LAMONT

In the ruins of Serondela you will find the grave of 'Pop' Lamont, next to the remains of his old house. 'Pop' Lamont was the last resident of **Serondela** and refused to leave when the park was declared. He held off his evictors at gunpoint until special permission was granted for him to see out the last years of his life on the river bank in the area he so loved.

Above: *A field worker tends tomatoes in a commercial plot just outside Kasane.*
Below: *The memorial stone to 'Pop' Lamont, Serondela's last resident.*

There are two gates into the national park from Kasane, one south of the river near the airport called Sedudu gate, which is the direct route to Ngoma gate some 65km (39 miles) to the west and onward to Savuti. The main gate is 2km (1.2 miles) west of Kasane on the main road through the village. Soon after this gate is a turn-off to the left through Sedudu Valley which joins the Ngoma road to the Nantanga Pans 20km (12 miles) away. There are several water holes along the Sedudu Valley road as well as many large dead trees; these died when the valley last flooded. This is ideal terrain for seeing the area's considerable leopard population.

THE RIVER FRONTAGE

Along the 15km (9 miles) of river frontage between Kasane and the remains of Serondela the road branches into numerous loops, many of them following the river floodplain and offering some of the best game viewing to be found in Africa. The road network is well-developed and maintained and the concentrations and variety of game, especially in winter, are overwhelming. It is possible to negotiate most of these tracks in two-wheel-drive vehicles, although you are likely to scrape the bottom of your vehicle in some places. The Game Scouts at the main gate recommend that you stick to the main roads.

Shortly after the national park's gate is the turn-off to the luxury Chobe Chilwero Lodge followed within a few kilometres by the Chobe Game Lodge, made famous as the honeymoon venue of international film stars, Richard Burton and Elizabeth Taylor.

Serondela ★★★

Serondela, 15km (9 miles) upstream from the main entrance to the national park, started its life in the 1930s as a veterinary camp and timber mill. Considering the denuded landscape in this area now, it is hard to imagine that just 60 years ago Serondela was covered with tall **teak forests** that supported a milling industry. Much of the marginal floodplain between Kasane and Serondela is now covered in dense green groves of **feverberry** (*Croton megalobotrys*) and woolly **caper bushes** (*Capparis tomentosa*), encroaching on the roads beneath the last remains of the tall and very dead white-wooded trunks of the former forest. The seeds of the feverberry tree are very effective in the treatment of malaria, hence its name, while the long arched branches of the woolly caper bushes provide perfect shelter for both lions and leopards, so don't consider leaving your vehicle.

Between Kasane and Serodela there are very high concentrations of game and one is almost guaranteed to see some of Chobe's 120,000 elephant – as well as buffalo and lions. The bird life is astounding and you are likely to see an array of unusual water birds including the amazing African skimmers (*Rynchops flavirostris*).

There used to be a national parks camp site at Serondela overlooking the river, but this has been moved to Ihaha where there are significantly upgraded facilities including hot showers and flush toilets and a very attractively designed reception office.

THE ELEPHANT DEBATE

The Chobe area contains the highest concentration of elephant in the world, with a total population, according to a 2004 estimate, to be about 120,000 individuals. There is massive pressure on the local natural resources to sustain such large populations of these leviathans, which is why there is such bitter debate about the validity of CITES and the ban on elephant hunting in southern Africa. Whatever the outcome of this argument the Chobe National Park is still the best place in the world to see the majestic African elephant.

Below: *A herd of buffalo fills the Chobe floodplain.*

Above: *The majestic sable antelope whose horns provide excellent protection against lions.*

At Ngoma Gate there is a private camp site, **Buffalo Ridge Camp Site,** which has reasonable facilities and offers travellers an overnight option on the long journey between Kasane and Savuti. The beautiful **sable antelope** (*Hippotragus niger*) are often seen in this Ngoma Gate area, while in late winter they tend to spread out along much of the river frontage towards Serondela.

Over 440 bird species have been recorded along this riverine section of the park, including many water birds such as the **malachite kingfisher** and the strangely beaked **African skimmer**. Chobe is also famous for the huge colonies of bright **carmine bee-eaters** which nest in the vertical river banks and can be seen in their hundreds acrobatically hawking insects over the river throughout the summer months

NOGATSAA AND TCHINGA

This pan-speckled grassy woodland lies some 70km (42 miles) due south of Serondela near the eastern park boundary. After the rains the pans hold water for several months making this area one of the finest game-viewing regions in the country.

Nogatsaa Camp Site ★★

The main camp site is at Nogatsaa Pan near the Game Scout Camp, where the facilities include water stands and basic ablutions. There is a lookout hut at Nogatsaa Pan and water is pumped here as well as at **Namuchira Pan** and at **Tchinga Pan** where the second camp site is located. These pans attract a large number and great diversity of game, particularly from August to October when elephant breeding herds concentrate near the water holes, although there can be unpleasantly strong winds in August and September.

This part of the national park is the best place to see Africa's largest antelope, the eland (*Taurotragus oryx*), which stands almost 2m (7ft) tall. Other animals often seen here include sable, leopard and cheetah.

Tchinga Camp Site ★★
The facilities at the **Tchinga camp site** are similar to those at the main camp, as is the lions' habit of stalking past the tents at night. While this can be very exciting, be cautious of these carnivores who wouldn't hesitate to attack. **Never** consider sleeping out of a tent under the stars.

Routes to Nogatsaa
There are two routes to Nogatsaa from Kasane, although the road through Sedudu Valley is extremely sandy. The recommended route is from Nantanga and is just under 50km (30 miles), but take great care in the rainy season as the area around Nogatsaa is black cotton soil which, when wet, is virtually impassable.

Ngwezumba Dam ★
Ngwezumba Dam no longer holds much water, its wall having been washed away by the drought-breaking rains in 1988. However, it can still offer very rewarding game viewing of the wildlife found in the area. The road past Ngwezumba goes on to Savuti some 114km (69 miles) away via the complex of pans at Zweizwe.

SAVUTI ★★★
This famous corner of the Chobe National Park has been hailed as Africa's prime wildlife area. The annual zebra migration passes through it; sightings of leopard, cheetah and wild dog are not uncommon; and it is here that you'll find the greatest concentration of that king of all beasts, *Panthera leo*.

MARAUDING ELEPHANTS

The public camp site in Savuti has had a chequered history. The old site was destroyed by thirsty elephants in their search for water. The new site has 'elephant-proof' taps, but the ablution blocks are less challenging for these giants, reputedly among the largest elephants in the world. Because of the possibility of elephant damage to the water supply it is vital that campers carry sufficient supplies of emergency drinking water.

Below: *A cluster of elephants enjoy a late afternoon drink at the river.*

RARE ANTELOPE

The Chobe National Park is the only place you are likely to see several very rare species of antelope. They include:

Chobe bushbuck *(Kobus ellipsiprymnus)* – Unique to this area these beautiful bushbuck are slightly redder than the more common Southern and East African species. These animals can be seen in the evenings under the woolly caper bushes between Kasane and Serondela.

Puku *(Kobus vardoni)* – Similar to impala, they are however slightly smaller and redder lacking the distinctive markings of the impala and lechwe with whom they often associate.

Oribi *(Ourebia ourebi)* – Similar to steenbok with a whiter belly. These rare animals are the world's smallest grazing antelope and can be seen grazing on new grass in recently burnt areas.

Sharpe's grysbok *(Raphicerus sharpei)* – Smaller and darker than steenbok these secretive, nocturnal animals can live close to human habitation and can be seen in the cultivated lands or plots in and around Kasane.

The main attraction of Savuti is the abundance of game and predators to be seen; at any time of year the sizes of herds can be staggering, while sightings of lion and hyena are almost guaranteed.

The Savuti area covers almost 5000km^2 (1900 sq miles) in the southwestern corner of the park, encompassing the Savuti Marsh, which is now a vast open plain, the Mababe Depression and the Magwikwe Sand Ridge.

Northern Botswana is at the tail end of the active Great East African Rift Valley and the region is traversed by numerous deep fault lines which can be seen in the sharply changing river courses.

Savuti Marsh ★★★

This marsh is originally what attracted the vast numbers of game to Savuti, providing an unlimited supply of water and rich pastures in an otherwise arid landscape. The game settled permanently in the area as did their predators and the lion and hyena populations grew dramatically, sustained by limitless prey.

According to the reports of early explorers the Savuti Channel filling the marsh flowed regularly between 1850 and 1880. It then suddenly dried up for almost 80 years before flowing again in 1957. This flow continued almost until 1982 when it once again inexplicably stopped.

To explain this flow, which is quite unrelated to the volume of the Linyanti River, geologists have measured

Right: *Hippos wallow in a pool in the Savuti Channel.*

the drop along the course of the Savuti Channel which is just a tiny 1 in 5300 over its entire length. After years of study many experts now believe that in order to stop the flow of the river the ground level of the Mababe Depression must be raised by as much as 9m (30ft) by the continual heaving and buckling of the faults in the area. For the river flow to change so frequently the ground must be in continual motion.

Above: *Impala, Botswana's most common antelope.*

Most of the camp sites in Savuti are along the banks of the channel overlooking a very noticeable line of dead camel thorn (*Acacia erioloba*) and knobthorn (*Acacia nigrescens*) trees that stand like gaunt sunbleached sentries along the length of the dry riverbed. These distinctive trees are flood victims, drowned when the river started flowing again in the 1950s. Their mature height shows that the channel must have been almost completely overgrown by that stage.

With the final drying of the Savuti Marsh, it has changed from a perennial wetland to semidesert in just a few short decades. Even the natural water table has dropped without the replenishment of the marsh, and the route of vehicles is now marked for miles around by the billowing black dust that drifts behind them.

Fortunately there are many natural pans in Savuti which hold water into the winter months, after which the animals must rely on the three pumped water holes, which see ever-increasing concentrations of game as other supplies dry up. In the last months before the rains (September and October) visitors must contend with soaring temperatures, but boreholes provide some splendid game viewing with droves of elephants, kudu, impala, buffalo, wildebeest, sable, lion, hyena, and the occasional cheetah vying for a chance to drink.

THE GROUND HORNBILL

The massive glossy black, red-faced ground hornbill (*Bucorvus leadbeateri*) which stands over 1m (3½ft) high is common to this area. These birds are called 'Lehututu' in Setswana after their deep booming call which, when heard, is reputed to be a sign of rain. While these birds are not sacred, they are still treated with care by the local people who believe that if you harm a ground hornbill, its mate will hound you to your death, cursing you with its endless lamenting call. Ground hornbill nests are very seldom seen, usually made in holes in trees high off the ground or in rocky cliff faces where they are unlikely to be disturbed.

Below: *Thousands of zebra gather, ready to start their migration.*

When the rains return the pans fill and lush green grass carpets the plains. With the rains come the zebra, moving in their thousands down from Linyanti into the area of the Savuti Marsh and the Mababe Depression.

Mababe Depression ★

The Mababe Depression is edged by the Magwikwe Sand Ridge which traces a semicircular line for 100km (60 miles) to the north and west of the Savuti Marsh. This ancient feature, measuring 20m (65ft) in height and over 175m (540ft) in width, provides a gruelling challenge to drivers trying to cross it.

Gubatsa Hills ★★

The seven Gubatsa Hills, which rise almost 90m (280ft) above the flat landscape and overlook the mouth of the Savuti Channel, provide fascinating evidence of the once great Makgadikgadi superlake. The northeastern faces of these hills have been cleaved into almost vertical cliffs by the millennia of waves that have pounded them, while on their leeward side are piles of beach pebbles rounded by the water's action.

Bushman Paintings ★★

There are over 20 Bushman painting sites to be found in the rocky hills in Savuti. Most are badly faded, but the best, which depict a variety of recognizable game including a puff adder and a hippo, can be seen on the eastern side of **Bushman Hill**. These artworks have been dated at over 3000 years old. While it is generally not permitted to get out of your vehicle in the national park, one can do so at Bushman Hill and a rough track leads the way to the paintings. There is a very large baobab tree near Bushman Hill which is worth a visit.

Left: *In a field of golden grass the fingers of a dead tree trace across a Savuti sky.*

The sandy soils of the Savuti support a variety of grasses, especially in the marsh area, which is dotted with tiny 'islands' of feverberry bushes and the larger raintrees (*Lonchocarpus capassa*). To the south in the Mababe Depression there is less vegetation with the area being predominantly covered with scrub thornbushes. However, throughout the sandy soils of Savuti wild sage bushes (*Pechuelloeschea leubnitziae*) grow well, giving the area a distinctive and pleasant smell.

Routes to Savuti

Many travellers with the time to spare choose to drive **from Maun** through Moremi Game Reserve to Savuti and onto Kasane taking in the country's major tourist attractions. If you are considering this route exit Moremi at North Gate by crossing the bridge over the River Khwai. After passing a few tiny villages the road continues eastwards across very sandy terrain until you enter the park. Turn left at the first fork in the road and continue north until you reach the Mababe Gate where all visitors must register. 10km (6 miles) beyond this office is another fork in the road. Both routes lead to the Savuti camp site approximately 46km (28 miles) away. The road to the left is slightly longer and follows the sand ridge capped with its mantle of camel thorn and Kalahari apple-leaf trees, while the one to the right goes via the marsh across

---

THE ZEBRA MIGRATIONS

Botswana is the site of two separate zebra migrations. One is between **Linyanti** and **Savuti** with zebra arriving in Savuti in late November. They foal in Savuti and return to Linyanti between February and April. With the drying of Savuti, the zebra may change their migratory pattern as ultimately there won't be enough water to sustain them. The other lesser known migration occurs in the **Makgadikgadi**, but tragically the numbers of zebra in this migration were decimated during the drought of the 1980s. Their numbers have never recovered.

PEL'S FISHING OWL

The Linyanti swamp and the Okavango Delta are the best places to see the remarkable Pel's fishing owl (*Skotopelia peli*), although you are much more likely to hear their eerie wailing scream. These birds have a massive wingspan
of over 1.5m (5ft), giving them the strength to lift fish weighing over 2kg (4.5lb) straight out of the water. Most owls have feathered legs, but Pel's fishing owls have long scaly claws and rough soles for gripping their slippery prey. Their eyesight is highly developed, even compared with other owls, and at night they perch 1 to 2m (3 to 6ft) above the water studying the depths for fish, which form the majority of their diet. They also eat frogs, crabs, mussels and young crocodiles.

treacherous black cotton soil, making both alternatives extremely challenging. In the wet season go left, in the dry season go right. The total distance from North Gate to Savuti is 110km (66 miles).

From Kasane one can drive either via Serondela and Ngoma Gate or via Nogatsaa and around the Savuti Marsh. The road via Serondela is approximately 170km (100 miles) and is direct, leading out of the park at Ngoma, past the villages of Kavimba and Kachikau on the edge of the Liambezi floodplain, though deep sand dunes can hamper your progress. The road then takes you back into the park cutting directly southwest to the camp site.

From Nogatsaa take the road to Ngwezumba Dam, and then follow the track along the river course for a full 120km (72 miles) before you reach Savuti, marked by Quarry Hill with its huge distinctive baobab tree nestling next to it.

LINYANTI ★★★

In the furthest corner of the Chobe National Park lies the forgotten paradise of Linyanti. Secluded and uncrowded, this short strip of swampy river frontage is reminiscent of the Okavango's permanent waterways with papyrus-lined lagoons, reedbeds and a towering canopy of trees.

The Linyanti Swamp covers an area of almost 900km² (340 sq miles), which follows the river and fills the area between the converging courses of the Kwando and Linyanti rivers. The national park only touches the river for a short section on the far eastern edge of the swamp.

The wildlife is plentiful, especially in the dry winter months when great concentrations of elephant, buffalo, and zebra congregate along the river, with giraffe, impala and the unusual roan antelope being seen in the forests. The bird life is diverse, if not overwhelming in its numbers. Water birds, including pelican, are common while you are likely to hear, if not see, Pel's fishing owl.

The wilderness areas around the park have for many years been hunting concessions making the game, even within the park boundaries, wary and shy of humans.

The operators of these hunting areas have stated their intention to reduce the seasonal hunting activities and concentrate more on photographic safaris. If this happens the quality of game viewing will improve, and in the hunting season (April to September) visitors will not be disturbed by the sound of distant gunshots.

Linyanti Camp Site ★★★

The remote public camp site at Linyanti is possibly the most attractive to be found in Botswana, set in deep shade overlooking the papyrus and reedbeds that line the river, where resident hippo can be heard grunting to each other. There are well-maintained ablutions which include flush toilets and hot showers.

Outside the Chobe National Park along the river are several private camps which offer luxury tented accommodation and have their own private landing strips making access easier. Being outside the park, night drives and game walks can be arranged from these camps.

Routes to Linyanti

One can drive to Linyanti from either Savuti or Kasane, but both roads traverse patches of deep sand.

From Savuti take the Kasane road until you see a signposted turning to Linyanti on the left just before the water hole and landing strip. After 8km (5 miles) there is a fork where you bear to the right and continue straight for approximately 30km (18 miles) until you reach Linyanti.

From Kasane, take the Savuti road via Ngoma Gate and Kavimba until you reach the Chobe National Park sign where the road re-enters the park. Turn right here and follow the straight firebreak cutline for about 35km (21 miles) until it reaches the river where the Linyanti entrance gate is. The camp site is about 5km (3 miles) beyond the gate.

THE SAUSAGE TREE

This massive tree (*Kigelia africana*) which grows up to 20m (65ft) high is one of Africa's most distinctive, recognizable by its huge sausage-shaped fruit which can be seen any time between March and December. The large bright red flowers which adorn the trees from October to December are highly sought after by monkeys, baboons, antelope, civets, porcupines and, particularly, by Peter's epauletted fruit bat (*Epomophorus crypturus*). The fruit, although not widely consumed, contains steroids and is used in traditional medicine as a treatment for ulcers and rheumatism while in Zimbabwe it is being commercially marketed as a treatment for skin cancer.

Opposite: *The rare and fascinating Pel's fishing owl.*
Below: *A log bridge over the Savuti Channel.*

Below: *The buffalo is a formidable creature and is considered to be one of the most dangerous animals in the African bush.*

KAZUNGULA ★★

This small riverine village is named after a huge sausage tree (*Kigelia africana*) – 'Mzungula' in the local tongue – which until recently could still be seen growing on the river bank overlooking the confluence of the Zambezi and Chobe rivers. The tree was made famous in the diaries of David Livingstone who camped beneath it in 1855, the night before he discovered the Victoria Falls. This settlement, situated in the furthest northeastern corner of Botswana, has grown up around the border post and the river ferry mainly in order to service the needs of travellers and tourists passing through.

Basic supplies are available at Kazungula including petrol. Accommodation and camping facilities can be found at Kubu Lodge on the edge of the village towards Kasane from where boat trips to both the confluence or Chobe National Park can be arranged. Half way along the 12km (7 mile) road to Kasane are banana plantations, and opposite them towards the river is a noticeably barren patch of land ringed by dead trees. This is a salt seep whose mineral rich springs attract both elephant and buffalo. The seep developed in the early 1990s as a result of the plantation irrigation raising the local water table.

There is a good tarred road to Nata, 320km (192 miles) away through dense stands of forest. As the unfenced boundary of Zimbabwe's Hwange National Park is a short distance to the east of the main road for much of the way between Pandamatenga and Kazungula, there is

a good chance of seeing roan antelope, giraffe and elephant. Kazungula is Botswana's only border with Zambia and a vehicle ferry shuttles across the confluence between the two countries. At Kazungula travellers can cross into Zimbabwe and with the majestic Victoria Falls only 80km (48 miles) away on a good tar road, one can make easy day trips from Kasane to visit this natural wonder.

VICTORIA FALLS ★★★

To witness the falls stretching across almost 2km (5600ft) of sheer basalt cliffs with water crashing down over 100m (328ft) into the chasm below is definitely an unforgettable experience.

The many activities at the Victoria Falls include **white-water rafting**, which is reputed to be one of the safest and most exciting grade five runs in the world, as well as one of the world's most dramatic **bungi jumps** off the Railway Bridge into the churning 'boiling pot' a couple of hundred metres below.

Above: *Sunrise over the spectacular main falls.*
Below: *Bungi jumping: the fastest way into the boiling pot!*

Routes to the Victoria Falls

A good route for day visitors from Botswana is to cross into Zambia on the car ferry from Kazungula and drive to the Victoria Falls via Livingstone, then leave your vehicle at the Mosi oa Tunya Hotel while exploring the Zambian side of the falls.

Having explored the Zambian side go through the Customs post and cross the original 1905 bridge that spans the neck of the second gorge. The well-maintained paths through the dense rainforest lead from **Devil's Cataract** and **Livingstone's statue** along the front of the falls, passing the **Main Falls**, **Horseshoe Falls**, **Rainbow Falls**, and finally to the open rocky platform at Danger Point.

There are numerous good hotels on both sides of the Falls where one can enjoy lunch, followed by a visit to the crocodile ranch or the Big Tree, a cruise up the Zambezi, a game drive or a round of golf at Elephant Hills before returning to Botswana.

Your passport and visas must be valid for Zimbabwe and Zambia and remember that the Kazungula border post closes at 18:00 so you must leave the Falls by 16:30.

Chobe National Park at a Glance

BEST TIMES TO VISIT

The **game viewing** throughout the Chobe improves as the pans dry up and the game concentrates around the permanent water sources such as the river or the pumped water holes, with **August** to **October** being considered the best times to visit. Game viewing is good along the Chobe riverfront throughout the year, but the Mababe Depression and the Savuti Channel are usually inaccessible or closed during the **wettest months** from **December** to **March**. The summers can be uncomfortably hot, while in winter the early mornings, particularly in Savuti can be very cold. Strong unpleasant **winds** are also known to sweep across the Nogatsaa area in **August** and **September**.

GETTING THERE

There is an international airport at Kasane with regular **Air Botswana** flights from Gaborone and Maun. There are landing strips at both Savuti and Linyanti which service the private camps in those areas.
There is a good tar road to Kasane from Francistown, while there are four-wheel-drive only routes to Savuti from Maun and Moremi. From Zimbabwe and Zambia the best route is via Kazungula, while from

Namibia entry is via Katima Mulilo at the Ngoma Bridge border post. There is no rail link to Kasane, although there is an exclusive **Blue Train** rail safari that occasionally incorporates Chobe. It drops passengers off at the Victoria Falls; they are then flown to Kasane and, after a round of game drives, fly on to Francistown where they reboard the train which returns to Johannesburg in South Africa.

GETTING AROUND

There are numerous safari operators in Kasane and all the lodges are able to arrange airport collections, game drives and boat trips for both guests and casual visitors. For those who prefer unguided trips, there is an **Avis** Rent-a-Car office at Mowana Safari Lodge, tel: 625-0144, fax: 625-0469, from where appropriate four-wheel-drive vehicles can be hired. Pre-booking of Avis vehicles can be done through any international travel agent.

WHERE TO STAY

There are many excellent lodges, hotels and luxury camps in the Chobe area, and with the concession system of land allocation for tourism operators in Botswana, new ones are being established all the time, so it is important to consult your travel agent who can recommend options that

will suit your needs, wants and budget.

Kasane
Chobe Marina Lodge, tel: 625-2221, fax: 625-2224. In a beautiful setting on the banks of the Chobe river.
Chobe Safari Lodge, tel: 625-0336. Offers a range of accommodation including camping, plus a restaurant, pool and shops.
Elephant Valley Lodge, tel: 625-0992, fax: 625-1297. Luxury tented lodge with excellent restaurant.
Impalila Island Lodge, tel: 625-0794. New luxury lodge with great cuisine and river cruises.
Mowana Safari Lodge, tel: 625-0300, fax: 625-0301, e-mail: resmowana@cresta. co.bw Stunning architecture and setting with over 110 rooms and a choice of restaurants.
Sedudu Guest House, tel: 625-0284. Small and personal.
The Garden Lodge, tel: 625-0051, fax: 625-0577, e-mail: gabi@thegardenlodge.com Idyllic setting with very good accommodation and restaurant.

Kazungula
Kubu Lodge, tel: 625-0312, fax: 625-1092, e-mail: kubu@botsnet.bw Famous for its restaurant and wooden cabins set in lush lawn on the river bank, plus well serviced camp sites.

Chobe National Park at a Glance

Pandamatenga
Muchenje Safari Lodge,
tel: 623-6000.

Serondela
Chobe Chilwero Lodge,
tel: 625-1362, fax: 625-1473,
e-mail: chilwero@info.bw
Beautiful river views,
outstanding food and
attentive highly qualified
game guides.
Chobe Game Lodge, tel:
625- 0340/1761. Long
established luxury hotel
with excellent facilities and
game activities.

Savuti
Allan's Camp, tel: (+27 11)
884-2504, fax: (+27 11)
884-3159. Reed and wood
chalets overlooking the
Savuti Channel.
Lloyd's Camp, tel: (+27 11)
453-7649, fax: (+27 11) 453-
7646. Luxury tented camp
with private hide overlooking
the camp's water hole.
Savuti South. A sister camp
to Allan's Camp with fully
equipped tented accommodation. Contact numbers are the
same as for Allan's Camp.

Linyanti
Kings Pool Camp, managed
by Okavango Wilderness
Safaris, tel: 686-0086, fax:
686-0632, e-mail: travelshop
@ows.bw Luxurious tented
suites overlooking the hippo
filled Kings Pool. Night drives
and double-decker boat trips
on offer.

CAMPING
There are National Parks
public camp sites throughout
the Chobe National Park; at
Ihaha where there are hot showers
just 15km (9 miles) from
Kasane; at **Savuti** where there
are special 'elephant-proof'
water points and showers; in a
beautiful shady forest setting
at **Linyanti**; at **Nogatsaa**
where there is also running
water, and there is a basic
camp site at **Nchinga**, but
facilites here are very
limited and campers must be
self-sufficient. There is also a
privately owned camp site at
Buffalo Ridge near Ngoma
Gate which has running
water and ablution facilities,
while there is a choice of
camp sites at the lodges in
Kasane and **Kazungula**.

Almost all of the above
lodges and camps have
restaurants offering excellent
cuisine, although most are
closed to the public (open to
residents only). Public restaurants are only available in
Kasane and Kasungula and
there are many of them. A
few of the finer ones include:

Chobe Safari Lodge,
tel: 625-0336. Casual
restaurant with bar; serves
good home-cooked meals.
Mowana Safari Lodge,
tel: 625-0051. The main
dinning restaurant serves
excellent local and international cuisine.
Kubu Lodge, located at
Kazungula, tel: 625-0312.
This lodge has a wooden
restaurant on stilts with an
open-air veranda overlooking
Mpalila island.

All of the private lodges and
camps offer their own game
drives as well as boat trips
(depending on their location).
Public trips from Kasane can
be arranged through one of
the following:
Afro Ventures, tel: 625-0119.
Organized overnight trips
across the national park as
well as game drives and
boat cruises.
**Blackbeard and Hepburn
Safaris**, tel: 625-1252.
Specializing in trips throughout the Chobe area.
Go Wild Photo Expeditions,
tel: 625-0289. General safari
operators based in Kasane.

KASANE	J	F	M	A	M	J	J	A	S	O	N	D
MIN AVE TEMP. °C	20	19	19	17	14	11	10	13	17	20	21	20
MIN AVE TEMP. °F	68	66	66	63	57	52	50	55	63	68	70	68
MAX AVE TEMP. °C	31	30	31	31	29	26	26	30	33	34	34	31
MAX AVE TEMP. °F	88	86	88	88	84	79	79	86	91	93	93	88
RAINFALL mm	141	138	71	19	1	0	0	0	1	28	51	142
RAINFALL in	5.6	5.4	2.8	0.7	0	0	0	0	0	1.1	2	5.6

8
The Okavango Delta

As the world's largest inland delta, the Okavango covers over 15,000km² (5700 sq miles) of lush verdant wetland. This unique area contains an incredible 95% of all surface water in Botswana and is one of Africa's prime tourist destinations. Surrounded by the parched Kalahari, this emerald jewel is an immense oasis fed by the flow of the mighty Okavango River which, unlike every other major river in the world, never reaches the sea but dies in the desert sands of northern Botswana.

The Delta is roughly cone-shaped and is approximately 175km (110 miles) in length from the apex to its base near Maun. It has given rise to a teeming variety of life, sustained by a myriad seasonally undulating waterways which provide an ideal environment for the plants and animals of the Okavango.

MAUN

Almost all tourists entering the Okavango do so through Maun, situated at the gateway to the Delta and Moremi Game Reserve. Maun is the tourism capital of Botswana and the administrative centre of Ngamiland. It is also the headquarters of countless safari and air-charter operations whose signs and offices dot almost every intersection, particularly towards the airport.

Since the town's establishment in 1915 as the tribal capital of the Batawana people, Maun has had a rough and ready reputation as a hard-living 'Wild West' town servicing the local cattle-ranching and hunting operations. But with the growth of the tourism industry and

DON'T MISS

★★★ A relaxing **mokoro ride** across the lagoons.
★★★ A **game viewing flight** over submerged floodplains.
★★★ **Exploring** hidden, uninhabited islands deep in the Delta.
★★★ Casting your line into the boiling waters of the annual **catfish run**.
★★ Sighting the rare aquatic **sitatunga** and **red lechwe**.

Opposite: *A mokoro drifts lazily through the water lilies of the Santa-dadibe River, deep in the Okavango wetlands.*

CLIMATE

The Okavango has a long dry winter from May to October with little or no rainfall. The days are warm and often cloudless, although the nights and early morning can be cold with temperatures near freezing. The majority of rain falls between December and February, and from November to April it can be oppressively hot and humid.

the completion of the tar road from Francistown in the early 1990s, Maun has developed rapidly, losing much of its old frontier town character. It is now home to almost 50,000 people.

Regular supplies of almost everything can be bought in Maun, and the town boasts several good shopping centres, filling stations, a choice of hotels and lodges as well as car and four-wheel-drive vehicle hire. The Maun International Airport, which was officially opened in 1996 after extensive renovations, is – if one counts the light aircraft charters to the various Delta camps – one of the busiest airports in southern Africa.

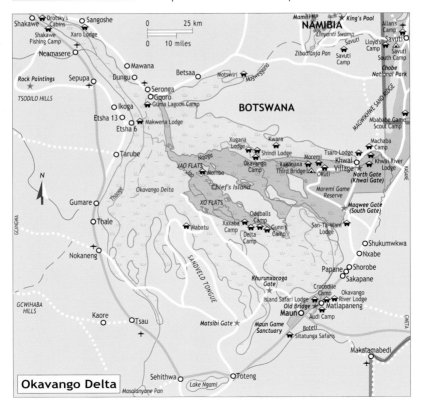

Okavango Delta

The name Maun is derived from the San word *maung* which means 'the place of short reeds' and this metropolis is now spread out along the wide banks of the timeless Thamalakane River where red lechwe can still be seen grazing next to local donkeys, goats and cattle.

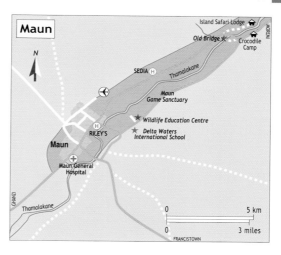

As one crosses the new causeway across the Thamalakane River to the main commercial centre, the famous Riley's Hotel is set on the river bank to the left of the main traffic circle. This fine hotel is a very popular stopover with tourists travelling into and out of the Delta, and has been an important landmark in the town since the 1920s when Charles 'Harry' de Beauvoir Riley first arrived here. In those days it was a gruelling 35-hour haul from Francistown to Maun and when the men (mostly professional hunters) arrived, all they wanted was something cold to drink and a place to relax. Seeing the opportunity, Harry set up a little bar that was the scene of many wild parties.

Another traditional watering hole, fondly remembered, was the **Duck Inn**, which has been replaced by the **Bull & Bush**, a popular extension of the famous Bull & Bush in Gaborone. The **Sports Bar** is another favourite drinking spot for both tourists and locals.

Other areas of interest in and around Maun include the small **Maun Game Reserve** which covers just 8km² (2.4 sq miles) of woodland. It follows the Thamalakane river bank upstream from Riley's Hotel and includes the original 'Place of Reeds' from which the town takes its name. The reserve is open every day and is traversed by numerous walking trails for which a small entrance fee is charged.

FACTS AND FIGURES OF THE OKAVANGO

Total river length – 1430km (872 miles).
Average sediment load – 650,000 tons per year.
Delta size – 15,846km² (6038 sq miles).
Delta composition:
Perennial wetlands – 4887km² (1862 sq miles);
Seasonal wetlands – 3855km² (1470 sq miles);
Seasonal grassland – 2760km² (1052 sq miles);
Intermittent flooding – 2502km² (954 sq miles)
Dry land – 1842km² (702 sq miles).

Above: *Modern Maun:
the 'Place of Reeds' on
the far left, the new
bridge, Riley's Hotel in the
trees and the commercial
centre in the distance.*
Opposite: *Moremi Game
Reserve's north entrance.*

THE SEASONAL FLOOD

The oscillating flow of water
across the Okavango Delta is
a timeless constant of rejuve-
nation and regeneration,
peaking in the parched southern reaches in the dry winter
months. The reason for this
abundance of water in what
is usually the dry season is
the distant rainfall in Angola;
it takes the floodwater a full
six months to wash through
the Delta. It reaches the
Panhandle in May, but slows
down in the flat sandy-
bottomed Delta until the
meagre unevaporated
remains reach Maun, usually
some time in August. The
arrival of the waters in Maun
is greeted with much local
excitement and every year
bets are made as to the exact
time and date of its arrival.

Maun Crocodile Farm ★★

The Maun Crocodile Farm has almost
4000 crocodiles penned in near-natural
surroundings. Open daily 09:00–18:00
Monday–Saturday, 10:00–17:00 Sunday.

Nhabe Museum ★★

The Nhabe Museum is community-based
and represents the people and culture of
northwestern Botswana. It can be found on the main road
near the airport turn-off. In addition, there are curio and
craft shops, including the Bushman Craft Shop near the
airport, the Leopard's Lair opposite the runway, Thuso
Curio Shop off the Toteng road and Mukwa Woodcraft, at
the Mukwa Leaf Gardens near the Sedia Hotel. Open
08:00–17:00 Monday–Friday, 11:00–16:00 Saturday.

Matlapaneng Bridge ★★

Just outside Maun on the road to Moremi, near the
turn-off to Crocodile Camp and Island Safari Lodge is
the old Matlapaneng Bridge, which has been preserved
as a National Monument. Going out of town take the
dirt track to the right just before the new bridge and
you'll cross the ancient calcrete and mopane pole
bridge. There is a pleasant picnic site on the eastern
side of the bridge next to the water hole.

There are many different people living in Maun
from the Batawana and the Bayei, to the Basubiya,
Hambukushu and the Mbanderu group of the Herero
people. This distinctive group of Herero live near the
centre of Maun at the turn-off to the old single-lane
bridge, where you are bound to see the flamboyantly
dressed women in their flowing Victorian outfits. If
you are tempted to take their photograph, it is important to ask permission first and to pay the women a fee
for the imposition.

The Francistown to Maun road is 492km (306 miles) of
good tar, as is now the road from Ghanzi to Maun. This
286km (173-mile) stretch was tarred in the early 2000s,
finally completing the circular road around Botswana.

MOREMI GAME RESERVE ★★★

Today Moremi is described as one of the most beautiful and varied reserves in Africa, with an unprecedented concentration of wildlife. But it has not always been so. By the end of the 19th century the wildlife in the southern Okavango had been practically exterminated by the rinderpest epidemic. It took many years for the game to regain its numbers and it was only with the return of the foot-and-mouth disease-carrying **tsetse fly** in the late 1940s that encroaching pastoralists were forced to move away. Uncontrolled hunting by European and Batswana hunters also took its toll and by the early 1960s much of the wildlife in this area had again been decimated.

Under the leadership of Mrs Moremi, the wife of the late Chief Moremi III, and with the help of Robert and June Kays and other early conservationists, the tribe agreed to set aside the far eastern corner of mainland between the Khwai and Mogogelo rivers as a wildlife reserve. The reserve was proclaimed on 15 March 1963 and was named after Chief Moremi III.

The Moremi Game Reserve now covers 4872km² (1856 sq miles). Moremi is only accessible by air or four-wheel-drive vehicle, and only the eastern side of the reserve is accessible by road as much of the central and all of the eastern side of the park is dense swampland. In the wet season many of the sand roads become impassable.

There are several private lodges along the old park boundary, but within Moremi there are only four public camp sites.

WHERE THE WATER GOES

The huge mass of water in the Okavango Delta represents 95% of all surface water in Botswana, but with a giant surface area, shallow depths and high daytime temperatures, 96% of it is lost to evaporation, 2% is absorbed into the underground water table while a mere 2% drains into the Thamalakane River. With water being such a scarce and valuable resource, in Botswana there have been many utilization plans to tap the Okavango's waters, while others in Angola and Namibia also claim rights to the water. However, environmentalists have proven that even a fractional reduction in the average flow will cause the destruction of unique flora and fauna in the southern floodplains. Both the International Union for the Conservation of Nature (IUCN) and Green Peace have studied the sensitive ecology of the Delta and are now lobbying for this wetland area to be declared a World Heritage Site.

South Gate Camp Site ★★

This camp site is set in a clean open, but grassless area under tall mopane trees, right at the **Maqwee Gate**. With a couple of ablution blocks equipped with boilers for hot water, it is an ideal site for those arriving at the gate late in the afternoon who would be unable to reach any of the other sites before the closing time when driving is no longer permitted.

GUARDIANS OF THE DELTA

Tsetse fly (*Glossina morsitans*) are endemic to the Delta and, as the carrier of both the feared **African sleeping sickness** in humans and foot-and-mouth disease in cattle, there have been numerous attempts to exterminate these parasites, including slaughtering all the wildlife that provide a possible food source for the flies, chopping down all the acacia trees which provide shade for them, and, more recently the blanket aerial spraying of DDT over the entire Delta. None of these destructive methods has worked and now the Tsetse Fly Control Department has devised a more effective and environmentally friendly system of 'flag' traps. The numbers of these insects are now greatly reduced but if you are nipped be thankful that they are still there to stall the encroachment of the hungry herds of cattle.

Right: *The fearsome crocodiles found in the Delta can grow up to 6m (19ft) in length and weigh over a tonne.*

Third Bridge Camp Site ★★★

The popular Third Bridge Camp Site is situated 50km (31 miles) northwest of Maqwee Gate. Approximately 40km (24 miles) from Maqwee the road crosses two old rickety mopane pole bridges which are predictably known as First Bridge and Second Bridge, and are the crossing point onto **Mboma Island**. Third Bridge and its adjacent camp site are a further 10km (6 miles) along the main track. The site is shady and idyllically situated on the edge of a permanent, clear lagoon. This clean water is safe to drink but do not consider swimming as there have been attacks by **crocodiles**.

The site includes barbecue areas, rubbish pits and ablution blocks with hot showers – although you may have to light the boiler fires to heat the water. Third Bridge is renowned for its lions which often walk through the camp at night. **Note:** even if you don't hear these predators, be sure to avoid wandering about unnecessarily after dark.

Fourth Bridge is 6km (3½ miles) beyond Third Bridge and is near a series of pools and pans, including **Botelele Pool** which attracts vast numbers of animals and birds and has its own resident hippos and some big crocodiles. The **Dobetsaa Pans** are to the south of the bridge and are one of the few places in the park where one is likely to see the remarkable **African skimmer**. Pelicans are sometimes seen at **Maya Pan** on the way to Xakanaxa.

Xakanaxa Lagoon ★★★

Xakanaxa Lagoon, which boasts some of the widest varieties of fish to be found anywhere in the Delta, is some 12km (7 miles) north of Fourth Bridge and is a vast expanse of deep, permanent reed-lined waterways. Several private camps and lodges have been established along the edge of the lagoon including **Camp Moremi**, **Camp Okuti** and **Xakanaxa Camp Site**. Just outside these lodges is a small shop selling basic provisions. This is the only area in Moremi where boats and canoes can be hired.

Xakanaxa Camp Site ★★

Xakanaxa Camp Site is just after the lodges, spread out on a thin strip of dry land between the Xakanaxa lagoon and a dense wetland reedbed. The site has ablution blocks with hot showers and a slipway to launch boats.

Above: *Real fan palms silhouetted against the setting sun.*

Nyandambesi Lediba and Dombo Hippo Pool ★★★

It is a long journey of almost 45km (27 miles) from Xakanaxa to North Gate where the fourth camp site is located, and it is worth breaking this trip with a visit to **Nyandambesi Lediba** and the **Dombo Hippo Pool** on the way. Nyandambesi Lediba, which means 'the lagoon where you can barbecue catfish', is an open series of pools and is less than 10km (6 miles) from the Xakanaxa camp site. At Dombo Hippo Pool there is an observation hide which is signposted and which can be found a short distance off the main Xakanaxa/Khwai road, some 12km (7 miles) from Khwai.

North Gate Camp Site ★★

North Gate Camp Site is situated under shady trees directly after the North Gate bridge on the banks of the **Khwai River** opposite Khwai village. The usual camping facilities are here, while there are one or two small rural stores in Khwai village selling only the most basic

MAKING THE MOKORO

The mokoro is the principle means of transport for the people of the Okavango, but with the growing demand for these craft at the many camps and lodges their production has become commercialized. The production is a long and painstaking process which takes several weeks and requires a long 'soaking' period where the boat is submerged to stop it drying out. There is thus grave demand on the Delta's slow-growing hardwoods and throughout the central Okavango the stumps and chopped remains of these trees can be seen. As a result most of the camps now use fibreglass mekoro.

commodities. Be aware that the monkeys in Khwai will steal anything they can from the moment you arrive. Therefore ensure that your tents and vehicle windows are closed at all times, and that foodstuffs are kept locked up in your vehicle away from the frustrating little thieves.

There are several lodges and camps in the Khwai area on the northern river bank outside the game reserve, such as **Tsaro Lodge**, the famous **Khwai River Lodge**, and **Machaba Camp** which is further along the Chobe road. All offer excellent game drives into the area. Khwai is well known for its concentrations of **elephant** and large herds of them can be seen towards the late afternoon heading down to the river. All of the loop roads that skirt the river banks offer the chance of rewarding elephant sightings.

Routes into Moremi

From the 'Bridge over the River Khwai' it is just 22km (13.5 miles) to the Chobe National Park boundary. For those going back to Maun there is a direct road from Khwai to Maqwee which cuts straight across the mopane woodlands for 30km (18 miles), but this road is challenging in the wet summer months.

There are **airstrips** at both Khwai and Xakanaxa, but most visitors to Moremi drive in from either Maun or Savuti. From **Maun** the road is tarred up to the village of **Shorobe**. There are a few little shops in this village, but no petrol, and from here the road is gravel for the

Below: *Tourists in a mokoro glide quietly across the waters.*

next 11km (7 miles) up to the Buffalo fence. This is the boundary to the wildlife management area that surrounds Moremi and the road degenerates dramatically from here onwards, making four-wheel-drive essential. A short distance beyond the Buffalo fence the road forks. **Maqwee Gate** into Moremi is 34km (21 miles) from this junction on the left-hand fork, while the right-hand

Left: *Red lechwe graze near the edge of a palm-lined waterway.*

fork is the road leading to Savuti and Kasane. One should allow around three hours to complete the 95km (58 mile) journey from Maun to South Gate.

The Bukakhwe San Bushmen's Gudigwa Camp ★★★

In the early 2000s one of southern Africa's most ancient and vulnerable communities, the Bukakhwe San Bushmen with the help of Conservation International and Okavango Wilderness Safaris launched Gudigwa Camp. This is a unique community-run ecotourism project that offers guests a first-hand insight into the rapidly disappearing San way of life, while preserving their traditional values and generating community income and employment.

Gudigwa Camp is located near the community's tribal village in the upper extremity of the Okavango Delta. The camp can host up to 16 guests in comfortable grass huts modelled on traditional San shelters. Through walking tours, community members teach guests about the ancient San cultural heritage including the use of medicinal plants, gathering water in the dry season, traditional storytelling, song and dance.

THE CENTRAL AND SOUTHERN OKAVANGO

The permanently and seasonally flooded areas within the central and southern Okavango hide within their cloak of beautiful lagoons, backwaters and forested islands some of the finest safari camps in the world.

> **WHY THE HIPPO SCATTERS HIS DUNG**
>
> You will notice that both on land and in water hippos have a strange habit of scattering their dung with their tails. Local legend has it that when the world was young the hippo asked God if he could live in the lovely cool water. But God said no, because he was so big with such a huge mouth he would eat up all the fish. The hippo pleaded with God saying that he would never harm the fish and that he just wanted to be nice and cool. Eventually they agreed that the hippo could live in the water, but that he must scatter his dung so that from heaven, God can look down to see that there are no fish bones in it, just pure grass.

Right: *Guests enjoy a sumptuous dinner after their evening game drive at one of the Delta's luxury camps.*
Opposite top: *A walking safari led by a game guide wades through the shallow water between two islands.*
Opposite bottom:
A netted tigerfish displays the teeth and stripes which have earned it its name.

FISH OF THE OKAVANGO

There are between 60 and 70 different species of fish to be found in the Delta. In the fast-flowing rivers of the northern **Okavango** and **Panhandle** area the small fish seek shelter in the papyrus beds while the large predatory fish which include tigerfish, bream, sharptoothed catfish, striped robber and the long-tailed spiny eel hunt in the open waters. The clear nutrient-rich **lagoons** are vital spawning and breeding grounds for a multitude of fish including the redbreast tilapia, the thinface large-mouth, Zambezi grunter and the southern squeaker. While the **seasonal floodplains** which fluctuate between aquatic and terrestrial phases are also home to a rich variety of fish including the African pike, silver catfish, pink happy and the many-spined climbing perch.

Down the length of the Delta these safari camps offer visitors a range of activities. The northern and central camps tend to concentrate on aquatic activities such as fishing and mokoro safaris, while the southern camps offer terrestrial activities, such as game drives and walks.

Some camps outside the Moremi National Park boundary offer **night boat rides** to see the crocodiles and birds. The eyes of the crocodiles are highly reflective and it is terrifying to see just how many there are out there.

Xigera Camp ★★★
Xigera offers numerous activities including mokoro trips, extensive game walks, drives and, at times, fishing.

Elephant-back Safaris
Specialized establishments can be found in the Okavango offering anything from bird watching to elephant-back safaris. These elephant safaris, reputed to have been the first of their kind in Africa, were started at **Abu's Camp**.

THE PANHANDLE, TSODILO AND WESTERN OKAVANGO
Known as the Cubango, the **Okavango River** rises in the rain-drenched Bie Plateau in northeastern Angola, also the source of the Chobe, Congo and Zambezi rivers. From here it flows south gaining momentum as it courses across 1300km (800 miles) of Kalahari sand before changing its name to the Okavango when it crosses Namibia's Caprivi Strip and enters Botswana at Mohembo.

The Okavango River flows between two parallel faults which form a shallow valley just over 10km (7 miles) wide. Within this constriction, aptly known as the **Panhandle**, the river flows straight for 95km (59 miles). Then just beyond the tiny village of Seronga on its northeastern bank, the river crosses the **Gomare Fault**, which releases it to spill its waters into the huge Delta.

Shakawe ★★★

Since the early 1990s, the Panhandle has become more accessible with the tarring of the Maun/Shakawe road and with the establishment of numerous camps and lodges along the riverbank.

With the Panhandle being deep and fast-flowing it is ideal for both the fighting tigerfish and delicious bream. Seventeen species of fish can be caught here, and they are all prized by anglers.

Bird watching is also outstanding in the region's tall, shady, riverine forests, and many resident and migratory birds can be seen along the river.

A visit to the Panhandle would not be complete without an excursion to the Tsodilo Hills, and most of the camps in the Shakawe and Panhandle area can arrange either fly-in or four-wheel-drive day or overnight excursions to this incredible archeological gallery.

BE CONSIDERATE

If you are taking part in night excursions, please be sensitive to the wildlife and appreciate that the intrusion of a blinding spotlight can be very disturbing, especially to some of the sleeping birds who may take hours to find a suitable perch again once you have gone. Also don't encourage your boatman to feed the wildlife, especially the fish eagles. It is a dramatic thing to watch one of these powerful birds scooping a fish out of the water and many unthinking tourists like to try their hand at photographing these staged events, but the birds become dependant and over-feed, ultimately leading to their demise.

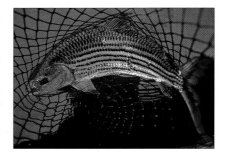

LEGENDS OF TSODILO

The Hills have a mystical presence and it is easy to believe the many legends of Tsodilo. The Hambukushu believe it is where God lowered man to earth, while the San believe that their various gods live in caverns within the Female Hill from where they rule the world, and it is they who will cause misfortune if anyone hunts or causes death near the Hills. The most sacred place is near the top of the Male Hill where the First Spirit knelt to pray after creating the world. This was when the rocks were still soft and if you look carefully you can still see the impression of his knees in the grey rock, while nearby there is a third impression where he placed his clay pot of cleansing water.

Below: *The bastion of the Tsodilo Hills towers over the surrounding plain.*

Tsodilo Hills ★★★

In the flat barren landscape of the western Kalahari, some 50km (31 miles) west of the village of Sepupa on the banks of the Panhandle, the sheer quartzite cliff faces of the four Tsodilo Hills rise abruptly out of the sand. In this haunting place evidence of ancient human habitation is rich. There are well over 3500 paintings charting 25,000 years of occupancy, making this one of the most important **rock art** sites in Africa.

There are four individual hills at Tsodilo. The tallest is known as the **Male Hill** and reaches up almost 400m (1310ft). Next to it is the **Female Hill**, behind which is a small hill called, predictably, the **Child Hill**. Beyond these three is a much smaller unnamed knoll, which legend has it was the Male Hill's first wife who was discarded when he met and married the taller Female Hill.

The track to Tsodilo Hills is extremely rough and suitable only for four-wheel-drive vehicles. The turning off the main Maun/Shakawe road is just south of Sepupa and is indicated with a National Museum signpost. There are no designated camp sites in the area and camping is permitted anywhere, but again, be sure to treat Tsodilo with respect.

There are several small villages on the main Maun/Shakawe road, some of which were settled by Hambukushu refugees who fled the war in Angola in the late 1960s. These people brought with them the skill of weaving and this area is now the centre of Botswana's most important craft industry – basket weaving.

Gumare ★★

The traditional village of **Gumare** is 260km (160 miles) from Maun. Because of its central location it was chosen as the site for the region's small hospital, and it is well worth stopping here on your way through to see the weavers and to buy their wares.

Left: *Papyrus fires are a common phenomenon in the delta with the peat banks bursting into flame at the slightest disturbance.*

Etsha 6 ★★★

The village of **Etsha 6** is the largest of the 13 settlements of Etsha and lies 30km (19 miles) north of Gumare. It boasts the only filling station between Maun and Namibia, as well as a couple of shops and the **Etsha Museum and Cultural Centre**. In Etsha 6 you will also find the **Okavango Basket Shop**. Open Monday–Saturday from 08:00–17:00. Just 14km (9 miles) away to the east, set in shady palms on the banks of an Okavango tributary is **Makwena Lodge**, making Etsha 6 an ideal overnight stop or holiday destination in itself.

Lake Ngami ★

Like the Makgadikgadi pans to the east, Lake Ngami is a relic of the superlake that once covered much of northern Botswana.

There are vast reedbeds on the edges of the lake, which die down to crumbling debris during the dry periods, only to regrow once the rains return. This cycle causes a bed of rotting vegetation to accumulate, making the waters of the lake extremely nutritious and attracting an array of birds. In good years the number of these water birds swells dramatically, accounting for the lake's reputation as the most prolific birding area in the world.

There are no tourist facilities at Lake Ngami, but for those with four-wheel-drive vehicles it can be an interesting excursion on the way to the Panhandle. There are various unmarked turn-offs to the lake, veering south off the main Maun/Shakawe road between Toteng and Sehitwa, which is 95km (58 miles) from Maun.

BUSHMAN PLACE NAMES

Many place names in Moremi are of Bushman origin; the sounds of this **San language** are difficult to pronounce:
x – a click, formed by sealing the tongue against the roof of the mouth and then sucking it down loudly.
q – made by pulling the tongue loudly away from the back of the front teeth.
xhl or **//** – produced by pressing the tongue against the teeth as if pronouncing the letter 'l', but instead, air is sucked in and the 'click' is pronounced at the back of the mouth, rather like the sound made to encourage a horse.

SMOULDERING EARTH

Lake Ngami has always been a mysterious place surrounded by legends and strange phenomenon, such as the smouldering earth around the lake flats that the local inhabitants believe is caused by the angry god, Lengongoro. The cause of this strange inextinguishable fire has vexed many. The real reason seems to be the **spontaneous combustion** of the deeply packed reedbeds that burn for months beneath the surface until the rains and floodwaters extinguish them.

The Okavango Delta at a Glance

Aug–Nov is considered to be the best, as after the first rains (can be in late Nov), the game rapidly disperses. Summer can be very hot but many of the animals have young which can provide fascinating viewing.

Air Botswana has regular flights to Maun from Gaborone and Johannesburg. All the camps in the Delta organize charter flights for their guests and these are usually frequent and timed to the Air Botswana arrivals. Some southern camps can be reached by boat, but with the papyrus obstructions and fluctuating water levels this needs to be arranged in advance. Few camps in the Delta can be reached by road, save for the camps in Moremi, Shakawe and along the western edge of the Okavango. Four-wheel-drive is essential off the main Maun/Shakawe road. Roads from Francistown and Ghanzi to Maun and Maun to Shakawe are good tar. The road on the eastern edge of the Okavango is very sandy and difficult even in four-wheel-drive.

The roads within Moremi are navigable by four-wheel-drive only and some are seasonal and may be submerged. Most camps in the Delta offer game drives and mokoro rides. While mekoro are the most common means of transport in the central and southern Delta, they are not recommended in the Panhandle where the river is fast flowing and crocodile infested. In this area stick to conventional boats.

There are many camps and lodges within the Okavango area with new ones being established all the time. Most camps are on land concessions that are not automatically renewed so they may be relocated. Hence use the following as a guideline only – check with your travel agent.

Maun
Audi Camp, 13km (8 miles) out of town on the Moremi road, tel: 686-3005. Camp site with bar, restaurant and pool.
Crocodile Camp, tel: 686-0265, fax: 686-0793, e-mail: sales@botswana.com Excellent restaurant and pool on the bank of the Thamalakane river near Audi Camp.
Island Safari Lodge, tel: 686-0300. Chalets, camping, bar, restaurant and swimming pool.
Maun Lodge, tel: 686-3939, fax: 686-3969, e-mail: maun.lodge@info.bw Comfortable and good value lodge in Maun.
Okavango River Lodge, tel: 686-0298. Comfortable accommodation, good restaurant.
Riley's Hotel, tel: 686-0320, fax: 686-0580, e-mail: resrileys@cresta.co.bw In centre of town, excellent restaurant and atmospheric Harry's Bar.

Sedia Hotel, tel/fax: 686-0177. Comfortable, good value, with camp site, restaurant and bar.
Sitatunga Camp, tel: 686-4539. Reed chalets, camp sites, shops and bottle store.

Central Okavango
Guma Lagoon Camp, tel: 687-4626, fax: 686-0571. Overlooking the lagoon; fishing, bird-watching, boating and walking.
Xugana Lodge, tel: 686-1805, fax: 686-1087. Reed and thatch chalets on stilts; game viewing and mokoro safaris.

Eastern Okavango
Gudigwa Camp, tel: 686-0086 (Okavango Wilderness Safaris), e-mail: travelshop@ows.bw web: www.gudigwa.com A unique ecotourism experience with grass shelters in a genuine San environment.
Khwai River Lodge, tel: (+27 11) 884-2504, fax: (+27 11) 884-3159. Luxury opposite North Gate on banks of Khwai.

Southern Okavango
Abu's Camp, tel: 686-1260, e-mail: ebs@info.bw web: www.elephantbacksafaris.com Famous for their elephant-back safaris.
Gunn's Camp, tel: 686-0023, fax: 686-0040, e-mail: gunns camp@info.bw Famous tented camp 'deep in the Delta'.
Kujwana Camp, tel: 686-1671, e-mail: ohsnx@info.bw web: www.okavangohorse.com Luxurious base camp for 5-

and 10-day horseback safaris across the southern Delta.
Oddballs Palm Island Lodge, tel: (+27 11) 788-5549, fax: (+27 11) 788-6575. Reasonably priced camping option with mokoro trails.

Moremi Game Reserve
Camp Moremi, tel: (+27 11) 789-1078, fax: (+27 11) 886-2349. Luxury camp with excellent cuisine and game viewing.
Camp Okuti, tel: 686-0570, fax: 686-1282, e-mail: okuti@info.bw 'A special African experience' at Xakanaxa lagoon.
San Ta Wani, tel: (+27 11) 884-2504, fax: (+27 11) 884-3159. Luxurious thatched chalets near Maqwee Gate.

Shakawe
Drotsky's Cabins, tel: 687-5035, fax: 687-5043, e-mail: drotskys@info.bw Beautiful riverside setting.
Shakawe Fishing Camp, tel: 687-5091, On banks of river, downstream from Shakawe.

CAMPING
Department of Wildlife and National Parks camp sites are at South Gate, Third Bridge, Xakanaxa and Khwai. All have basic facilities including showers and boilers for hot water. Book in advance at the Maun office, tel: 686-0368, fax: 686-1264.

WHERE TO EAT
Almost all private camps in the Delta serve outstanding cuisine but are all closed to the public.

The only restaurants and takeaways are in Maun and the following are just a few of them:
Bull & Bush, tel: 686-4250, fax: 686-4255. Based on the Bull & Bush in Gaborone.
By The Bridge, tel: 686-0435. Good food, generous portions.
Magic Lantern, tel: 686-1709. Restaurant and takeaway.
Sports Bar & Restaurant, tel: 686-2676. Popular bar, pub food, entertainment centre.
Steers, Ngami Centre, tel: 686-0918. International chain serving fast food and burgers.

TOURS AND EXCURSIONS
Travel agents and tour operators organize tours to almost anywhere in the Okavango, including elephant-back and horse-back safaris, helicopter tours and mokoro trails. For fishing safaris contact Okavango Fishing Safaris in Shakawe, tel: 687-5091/2.

USEFUL CONTACTS
Parks and Reserves reservations head office, tel: 318-0774, fax: 318-0775.
Avis Rent-a-Car, tel: 686-0039, fax: 686-1596, e-mail: avismun@botsnet.bw
Riley's Garage & Service

Station, tel: 686-0203, fax: 686-0556, e-mail: info@rileysgarage.co.bw

Safari Operators:
Abercrombie & Kent/ Sanctuary Lodges, tel: 686-2688, fax: 686-3526, e-mail: general@abercrombiekent.co.bw
Ker & Downey, tel: 686-0375, fax: 686-1282, e-mail: safari@kerdowney.bw
Okavango Wilderness Safaris, tel: 686-0086, fax: 686-0632, e-mail: travelshop@ows.bw

Air Charter Companies:
Delta Flyer, tel: 686-0569, fax: 686-0040, e-mail: deltaflyer@dynabyte.bw
Flying Mission, tel: 686-1456, fax: 390-4181, e-mail: hanger@flyingmission.org.bw
Kalahari Air Services, tel: 686-3816/7, fax: 686-3818, e-mail: kasmn@info.bw
Mack Air, tel: 686-0675, fax: 686-0036, e-mail: reservations@mackair.co.bw
Northern Air, tel: 686-0385, fax: 686-1559, e-mail: nair@kerdowney.bw
Sefofane, tel: 686-0778, fax: 686-1649.

MAUN	J	F	M	A	M	J	J	A	S	O	N	D
MIN AVE TEMP. °C	20	19	19	16	11	8	7	10	15	19	20	20
MIN AVE TEMP. °F	68	66	66	61	52	46	45	50	59	66	68	68
MAX AVE TEMP. °C	33	32	33	32	29	26	26	29	34	36	35	34
MAX AVE TEMP. °F	91	90	91	90	84	79	79	84	93	97	95	93
RAINFALL mm	112	105	62	27	3	1	0	0	5	19	48	82
RAINFALL in	4.4	4.1	2.4	1.1	0.1	0	0	0	0.2	0.7	1.9	3.2

Travel Tips

Tourist Information

All of Botswana's international embassies have tourism representatives from the **Ministry of Environment, Wildlife and Tourism**. They have large-scale maps and tourism directories which are available to the public. The Department's head office is in Gaborone's main Mall. For enquiries tel: 395-3024.

The **Department of Wildlife and National Parks** is responsible for the administration of all the national parks. Their head office is in Gaborone: PO Box 131, tel: 397-1405, fax: 391-2354. They also have an office in Maun, tel: 686-0368. Prepaid bookings for camping and entry into the northern parks must be made via this Maun office, and unbooked visitors will not be allowed in. For other camping bookings contact the Parks & Reserves Reservations (Gaborone), tel: 318-0774.

The **Hotel And Tourism Association of Botswana** (HATAB), tel: 395-7144, fax: 390-3201, e-mail: hatab@info.bw is a private organization with representatives from the tourism industry who promote the country in conjunction with the government.

There are several conservation societies and wildlife foundations in Botswana which provide information, such as:

Kalahari Conservation Society, tel: 397-4557. Promotes the conservation of the country's natural resources.

Chobe Wildlife Trust, tel: 625-0516. Aims to preserve the natural assets of the Chobe National park and northern Botswana.

The Botswana Society, tel: 391-9673. An historic humanitarian society which records the history and social development of the country

National Park and Game Reserve Opening Hours. Extended in 1996, the Park opening and closing times are:

January	05:30–19:30
February	05:30–19.30
March	06:00–19:00
April	06:00–19:00
May	06:00–19:00
June	06:30–18:30
July	06:30–18:30
August	06:30–18:30
September	06:00–19:00
October	06:00–19:00
November	06:00–19:00
December	05:30–19:30

Entry Requirement

Visitors to Botswana must have a valid passport and visa if necessary. Visas are not required for holders of South African, U.S. or E.U. passports. As regulations are subject to change, it is worth checking with any Botswana Embassy, Air Botswana or your travel agent if you will need a visa before you travel to Botswana.

Health Requirements

While Botswana is not a risky place to visit, certain precautions should be taken. Malaria, bilharzia and AIDS are main concerns but can be easily avoided. Tourists entering Botswana from southern African or western countries do not require inoculations, but vaccination certificates are necessary if you have recently been to a yellow fever zone. Piped water in urban Botswana is safe to drink and most tourist lodges and camps have reliable supplies, especially in the Okavango where the water is fresh and clean. But in the rest of the country check before drinking the water and when in doubt, boil all water before drinking. Health insurance should be organized before arrival in Botswana, as most camps and operators do not automatically cover their guests. Local MRI Medical Rescue and evacuation cover is recommended – contact MRI Medical Rescue, P/Bag BR256, Gaborone, tel: 390-3066, fax: 390-2117, e-mail: medrescue@info.bw

Getting There

By Air: Most fly-in tourists arrive in Botswana at either Gaborone or the tourist centres of Maun or Kasane which both have international airports. Pre-arranged charter flights can be made to most airstrips within the country, but an initial landing may have to be made at a larger airport where Customs and Immigration formalities can be cleared first.
By Road: There are almost 25 official crossing points into Botswana, from the busy Tlokweng border which is open 16 hours a day to the simple desk under the tree at the Chobe River mokoro taxi crossing. Road travellers usually enter at Tlokweng or Pioneer Gate from South Africa, Ramatlabama from Zimbabwe, Ngoma Bridge or Mamuno from Namibia, and Kazungula from Zambia.
By Rail: Travellers can get to Botswana by train, but the line only runs between Lobatse and Francistown, passing through Gaborone and the larger towns of the east, and does not link with any tourist destinations.

Customs

Customs regulations are subject to change so please treat the following as a guide only and confirm the current import limits before you arrive in Botswana with the Department of Customs & Excise (P/Bag 0041, Gaborone, Enquiries, tel: 364-2100, 392-2855, fax: 392-2781). Visitors are allowed to import 400 cigarettes, 50 cigars, 250g tobacco, 1 litre spirits, 2 litres wine and 300ml perfume. Botswana is part of a common customs area with South Africa, Namibia, Lesotho and Swaziland which means that products imported from these countries are not subject to import duty (although sales tax may be charged on certain items, including new clothing). Imports from other countries are subject to customs duty, though goods from Zimbabwe and Malawi do not require import permits. It is important to declare all valuable camera, optical and electronic equipment with the Customs upon arrival so that it can be easily taken out again with no questions about its origin.

Transport

Road: Although all the main centres in Botswana are now linked with good tar roads, the country still has a relatively limited road network which is still being developed. Secondary roads off these main arteries are generally gravel and mostly only suitable for four-wheel-drive vehicles. You may also find some primary roads in a poor state with potholes, especially after the

rainy season. Four-wheel-drive is necessary in almost all the national parks and game reserves in Botswana and these roads are not likely to be upgraded in the foreseeable future.
Driver's Licence: Always carry your original driver's licence and vehicle registration book with you. This is a legal requirement and if you cannot produce this paperwork you may face a long walk to fetch it!
Road Rules: In Botswana vehicles drive on the left and give way to the right, but take care as other drivers may not know this and can be unpredictable, especially minibus taxis which often stop in unexpected places. The general speed limit in urban areas is

60kph (36mph) while on the open road it is 120kph (72mph). Limits are strictly enforced and the police often set up radar speed traps, so do not be tempted to exceed the limit as the fines are high.
Car Hire: There are a range of car-hire companies:
Francistown: **Avis**, tel: 241-3901, fax: 241-2867; **Budget**, tel: 244-0083, fax: 241-8292; **Imperial**, tel: 240-4771/2.
Gaborone: **Avis**, tel: 391-3093, fax: 391-2205; **Budget**, tel: 390-2030, fax: 390-2028; **Imperial**, tel: 390-7233, fax: 390-4460.
Kasane: **Avis**, tel: 625-0144, fax: 625-0469.
Maun: **Avis**, tel: 686-0039, fax: 686-1596; **Budget**, tel: 686-3728, fax: 686-3563.
Petrol and Diesel: Petrol stations can be found along the major highways around Botswana and fuel is available 24 hours a day in the main centres, but have a full tank if entering from Namibia at Mohembo as the first filling station is only at Etsha 6. Petrol, diesel and unleaded petrol is available in Botswana.
Maps: Maps of Botswana are scarce, but a good national map highlighting the national parks is available from the Department of Tourism (P/Bag 0047, Gaborone, tel: 395-3024) and all international embassies, trade missions and Air Botswana offices. Shell Oil Botswana has produced excellent maps by Veronica Roodt, while the Globetrotter maps of Botswana are recommended and are available at the larger reputable bookshops in most

major cities. Detailed maps are also available from the Department of Surveys and Mapping in Gaborone, tel: 395-3251.

What to Pack
The dress code is casual in Botswana, particularly on safari, and even in the centres of Gaborone and Francistown few restaurants insist on a standard of dress. But do not wear camouflaged or military-style clothing as this, as well as topless or nude swimming is against the law in Botswana.
Note: internal flights within Botswana particularly to the camps in the Delta, Chobe and Tuli areas are generally in single or twin engine aircraft which have a strict **10kg baggage allowance**. If the flight is full any excess baggage will be left behind. Take only the essentials, i.e. lightweight summer clothing in neutral shades, long trousers and a long-sleeved shirt, track suit, warm jacket, comfortable walking shoes, hat, swimming costume, sunglasses, thick socks, sunscreen, malaria tablets,

insect repellent and a torch. A camera and bird-watching binoculars are also important. These should be packed into soft carry bags to ensure that they fit into the hold of smaller charter aircraft.

Money Matters
The currency in Botswana (Pula) is strong and easily exchangeable. It is divided into 100 thebe. Notes are in denominations of P100, P50, P20, P10 and P5. Coins are in denominations of P5, P2, P1, 50t, 25t, 10t and 5t.
Currency Exchange: Money can be exchanged at banks, hotels and bureaus de change.
Banks: Generally most banks are open from 09:00–15:30. Some banks close early on Wednesday and they are all closed by 11:30 on Saturdays.
Credit Cards: Visa, Mastercard and American Express are accepted by a variety of outlets and most hotels, lodges and safari operators will accept recognizable foreign currency and travellers' cheques.
Tipping: It is important to tip your mokoro poler, safari

CONVERSION CHART

From	To	Multiply By
Millimetres	Inches	0.0394
Metres	Yards	1.0936
Metres	Feet	3.281
Kilometres	Miles	0.6214
Square kilometres	Square miles	0.386
Hectares	Acres	2.471
Litres	Pints	1.760
Kilograms	Pounds	2.205
Tonnes	Tons	0.984
To convert Celsius to Fahrenheit: x 9 ÷ 5 + 32		

camp assistants, game ranger and guide and this can be done either at the time or as an extra when paying your bill at the end of your stay. While not mandatory, tipping is also expected in restaurants.

Accommodation

There is currently no grading system in Botswana, but the cost is often an indication of the standard of the establishment. The largest international hotel group is **Cresta Marakanelo**, tel: 391-2222, fax: 397-4321, e-mail: crestabs@info.bw which operates a range of hotels in Botswana. Other hotel groups represented in Botswana are the South African **Sun International** and **Peermont Global Hotels and Resorts** groups, each with one hotel in Gaborone.

There are numerous other **luxury lodges** and **safari camps** in Botswana's wildlife and tourist areas which offer outstanding accommodation, cuisine and service. Accommodation in these permanent safari camps is usually in large meru-style tents with tented or reeded en-suite facilities.

There are few **motels** in Botswana with just a couple being found in the towns along the major roads. **Self-catering** accommodation is available at some of the safari and rest camps, but facilities are rudimentary, generally being little more than a barbecue site. There are no youth hostels in Botswana, save for a **Y.W.C.A.** in Gaborone and, with the generally high cost of

---

PUBLIC HOLIDAYS

1 & 2 January
New Year
4 days, usually in early April
• Easter
1 May • Worker's Day
16 May • Ascension Day
1 July Sir Seretse Khama Day
15 July • President's Day
30 September • Botswana Day (Indepedence)
25 December
Christmas Day
26 December • Boxing Day

---

travel and low volumes of traffic, **backpacking** options are limited.

Camping is available at designated sites within the national parks and at privately owned sites throughout the country, but generally the facilities are limited. It is possible to camp in any public rural area, but be sure to ask permission from the local chief and be very careful to leave no litter or open fires behind. **Caravanning** is not an option in Botswana as most of the roads to the tourist areas are extremely rough and consequently there are no facilities for caravans even if you were able to get there.

Trading Hours

Most shops in Botswana are open from 08:30–17:00 during the week, and from 09:00–13:00 on Saturdays. In the more remote areas shops still follow the traditional hours, closing slightly later in the evening, but often shutting for

---

lunch. Government offices are open from 07:30–16:30 and are closed for lunch from 12:30–13:45, Mon–Fri.

Communications

Telephone and Fax: Botswana has one of the most sophisticated telecommunications systems in Africa. STD dialling is available to almost anywhere in the world (dial 00 to access the international satellite followed by the necessary codes). Public coin and card phones are available in most villages, while the remote camps are linked to their urban offices by radio. Phone cards are available at most large retail stores or post offices. Due to the sophistication of this network and the small number of users, telephone services in Botswana are expensive. Cellular phones are widely used throughout Botswana and there are two GSM cellular service providers; **Mascom**, tel: 390-3396 and **Orange**, tel: 316-3370. Both have roaming agreements with most countries and can provide temporary pre-paid numbers to visitors with their own handsets. The Botswana Telecommunications Corporation, tel: 395-8000, publishes a telephone directory for the country every year. There are hardly any fax agencies in Botswana, but almost all hotels offer a fax service to guests, and the larger establishments usually have full secretarial services available with e-mail and Internet access. There are Internet cafés in Botswana's main urban centres.

Postal Services: Even the remotest of villages usually has a post office and the service in Botswana is cheap and reliable, if somewhat slow.

Time

Botswana operates on Central African Time (C.A.T.) – two hours ahead of Greenwich Mean (or Universal Standard) Time, one hour ahead of European Winter Time and seven hours ahead of the USA's Eastern Standard Time.

Electricity

The power system in Botswana is 230V AC 50 Hz. Both round and square plugs are used so it is worth bringing adaptors for both. Lodges and camps in the tourist areas are generally not on the national power grid and rely on solar power or generators, which sometimes do not provide enough power for the use of hair dryers.

Weights and Measures

Botswana uses the metric system.

Medical Services

Pharmacies sell all necessary medicines and there is a list of private medical practitioners, hospitals and health centres in the coloured pages at the front of the telephone directory. **MRI Medical Rescue**, tel: 390-3066, offers a nationwide medical evacuation service to members, and the **Gaborone Private Hospital**, tel: 390-1999, is a fully equipped top-quality medical institution. Most tour operators do not provide clients with any insur-

ance and visitors are recommended to arrange their own health and travel insurance before arrival in Botswana, although it is well worth combining this with local MRI Medrescue membership.

Health Hazards

Malaria is endemic in northern Botswana and visitors should take the full course of anti-malaria tablets, before, during and after their trip. Although it is possible, the chances of contracting bilharzia are remote. **AIDS** is widespread, so avoid casual unprotected sex. After the first rains (Oct–Dec) in livestock areas there is a resurgence of **tick bite fever**. Insect repellent, long trousers and socks are a good deterrent, but check for ticks after walking through long grass. Tetracycline pills are effective in curing tick bite fever, but the full course must be taken. Hepatitis A has been recorded in Botswana. While infection is unlikely visitors can have Gamma globulin injections prior to arrival which offer six months protection against the disease.

Emergencies

In case of emergency dial 997 for an ambulance, 998 for the fire brigade, 999 for the police, and for MRI Medical Rescue members 911.

Security

Apart from licensed hunting rifles, guns are not available to the general public. Although there is the occasional armed robbery and with the close proximity of the South African

border to Gaborone, cars are sometimes stolen in the city, there is generally very little violent crime. Visitors should be aware of petty theft and pickpocketing and take sensible precautions, keeping cash and valuables locked away or out of sight. Bribery is frowned upon and the Directorate on Corruption and Economic Crime actively prosecutes anyone offering or accepting a bribe, so do not consider it. It is a male-dominated society in Botswana, so foreign women should be prepared for some conservative traditional attitudes, and unaccompanied women may also attract a degree of attention, particularly in the frontier towns. While the streets are generally safe in Botswana it is still worth using common sense.

GOOD READING

• A good bird reference book such as **Roberts' Birds of Southern Africa**, Gordon Lindsay, or **Newman's Birds of Southern Africa** and **Sasol Birds of Southern Africa**, Kenneth Newman.
• **Mammals of Botswana** (a field guide), Peter Comley and Salome Meyer,
• **Land Mammals of southern Africa**, Reay Smithers.
• **Signs of the Wild**, Clive Walker,
• **Trees of the Okavango Delta and Moremi Game Reserve,** Veronica Roodt.
• **Kalahari. Life's variety in dune and delta**, Michael Main.

INDEX

Note: Numbers in **bold** indicate photographs

agriculture 23, **24**
Aha Hills 10
aloes 39
Anglo-Boer War 37
antelope 96
archaeology 59

Bakalanga 25
Bakgalagadi 26
Bakwena 16
Bantu people 14, 27
baobabs 38, **59**
  Baines' Baobabs 62, **63**
  Baobab Trail 61–62
  Green's Baobab 62
Barbel Run 12
Basubiya 25, 26
Batawana 5, 107
Batswana 27
Bayei 25, 26
Bechuanaland 17
birdlife 12, 35, 36, 56, 91, 94
Bloem, Jan 40
Blue Jacket 55
Boteti River 59
Botswana Bird Club 33
Botswana Democratic Party (BDP) 18, 20
Botswana Meat Commission 24, 41, 55
British Council 33
British South Africa Company (BSAC) 17, 67
buffalo **93**, 102
Bukakhwe San Bushmen's Gudigwa Camp 127
bungi jumping **103**
Bushmen see San
butterflies 73

camel thorn tree **48**, 49
Cape to Cairo railway 31, 54, 67
Caprivi Strip 6, 8
cattle disease 25
cattle ranching 23–24
Central Kalahari Game Reserve **8**, 79–82
Chief's Island **11**, 116

Chobe National Park 5, 90
Chobe River **8**, 9, 53, **89**
CITES 23
climate 7–8
communications 125–126
crafts 34, 38, 40
crocodiles **112**
currency 8, 124
cutline grid 50

dassie **73**
De Beers 21
Deception Valley 80
Department of Wildlife and National Parks 23, 113
Devil's claw 79, 84
Devil's thorn **50**
diamonds 7, **21**–22, 82
Difaqane 15
Dombo Hippo Pool 113
donkey cart **38**
Drotsky's Caverns 10

economy 21–25
egrets, white **58**
elephant **67**, **95**
elephant-back safaris **22**, 116
Environmental Education Centre 35
Etsha 6 118

fishing 12, 36, 91, 116
flamingoes 57
food 29
Francistown 54–56

Gaberone, Chief 31
Gaborone 31–38
  Dam 36
  Game Reserve 34
  Yacht Club 36
Gallery Ann 34
Gcwihaba Hills 10
gemsbok **45**, 79
gemsbok cucumber 49
geology 6
Ghanzi 40, 49
gold 16, 22, 54, 55
government 20–25
grass seeds, danger of 81
Great East African Rift Valley 12

Great Zimbabwe Empire 14
Gubatsa Hills 98
Gumare 118
Gweta 60
  Rest Camp 60

Hambukushu 25, 26
health precautions 122, 126
Herero **24**, 27
hippopotamus 115
history 14–19
hornbill, ground 97
hunting 22

impala **97**
ivory 16

Jack's Camp 60
Jameson Raid 16, 17, 31
Jwaneng **20**, 21, 40, 47, 50

Kalahari 5, 6, **7**, 45, **48**, **79**, **81**
Kalahari Gemsbok National Park 45, 48
Kanye 40
Kasane 90–92
Kazungula 102
Kgalagadi Transfrontier Park **7**, 45–48
  pans 46–47
Kgale Hill 37
kgosi 18
kgotla 18
Khama, General Ian 83
Khama, Sir Seretse 17, **18**, 20, **31**, 33
Khama III Memorial Museum **83**
Khama III, Chief 67
Khama Rhino Sanctuary **83**
Khutse Game Reserve 84–86
  pans 84–85
Khwai River 113, 114
Kolobeng 39
Kubu Island 58–59
Kudiakam Dam 63

Lake Ngami 118
Lamont, 'Pop' 92
language 28
lechwe, red **115**
Lelhekane Mine 21

Lentswe-la-Oodi Weavers **38**
leopard **85**
Lepokole Hills 72
Letlhakeng 86
Limpopo River 41, 69
Linyanti 89, 99–101
lion **37**
Livingstone, Dr David 16, **17**, 28, 39, 40, 102
Lobatse 41
London Missionary Society (LMS) 16, **29**

Mabebe Depression 97, 98
Mabuasehube Game Reserve 45
Mafikeng 18
Mahalpye 74
Maitsong Theatre 34
Majale 69
Makabe, Chief 40
Makgadikgadi 5, 7, 11, 12, 53
Makgadikgadi and Nxai Pan National Park 60–61
manufacturing 25
Manyelanong Game Reserve 41
Mapungubwe Hill 14
Masetlheng Pan 50
Mashatu Cableway 70
Mashatu Game Reserve 68–71
Masire, Dr Ketumile 19
Mata Mata rest camp 48
Matlapaneng Bridge 110
Matsieng 38
Mauch, Karl 54
Maun 107–110
  Crocodile Farm 110
  Game Reserve 109
Missionaries' Road 79
Mochudi 36
Mokolodi Game Reserve 35, 36
Mokolodi Hills 35
mokoro **107**, **114**
Moremi III, Chief 5
Moremi Game Reserve **110**, 111–115
  Maqwee Gate 111, 114
  North Gate Camp Site 113
  South Gate Camp Site 111